The Diagnosis and Treatment of

Mental Illness

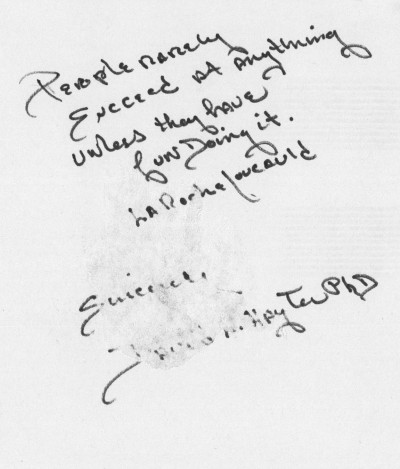

People rarely
Exceed at Anything
unless they have
fun Doing it.
LA Rochefoucauld

Enjoment!
David M. Hayter PhD

The Diagnosis and Treatment of
Mental Illness

AN INTRODUCTION

Jonathan P. Beard

David L. Hayter

Eric Shenkar

WAYNE STATE UNIVERSITY PRESS   DETROIT   1989

Library of Congress Cataloging-in-Publication Data

Beard, Jonathan P., 1956–
  The diagnosis and treatment of mental illness.

  Bibliography: p.
  Includes index.
  1. Psychiatry. 2. Psychology, Pathological. 3. Mental
health services. I. Hayter, David L., 1952–   . II. Shenkar,
Eric, 1956–   . III. Title.
RC454.B425 1989   616.89   88-5507
ISBN 0-8143-1920-3 (alk. paper)
ISBN 0-8143-1921-1 (pbk. : alk. paper)

To Kathryn, Erik, Diane, Sara, Brian, Jeanne, Betsy and our families for their continued support and encouragement throughout this endeavor

and to

Those individuals that this book is about, we express our deepest gratitude for all they have taught us

CONTENTS

8　　　　　　　　　　　　　　Contents

Contents 9

PREFACE

During the last few decades there has been a major new movement in mental health services. This new movement, deinstitutionalization, removes the emotionally disturbed from the state institution and places them into the community; it is the "emptying out" of state mental hospitals. Having begun in the 1950s with the introduction of psychotropic medications, by the 1980s deinstitutionalization matured into a serious social, political, and economic force.

Our intent is not to question whether deinstitutionalization is working, but rather to provide guidelines to individuals working with this perplexing and oftentimes difficult population. It has come to our attention that no book presently available has been written specifically for paraprofessionals concerning how to help emotionally disturbed individuals. Such a book is needed and in demand. Paraprofessionals are now in the forefront of the deinstitutionalization movement. Treating this disturbed and disturbing population requires both general and specific guidelines. It is our hope that such guidelines and treatment strategies are spelled out adequately in this volume and that these guidelines will be used with the best possible intentions. The book is intended to be used as a resource handbook for paraprofessionals working in hospitals, group homes, day treatment programs, work activity programs, and other programs involved in helping this population.

All of the situations and examples described in this book actually have occurred. However, all of the names and places have been changed in order to protect confidentiality. This

11

book was a collaborative effort by the authors. It represents
experiences from various sessions and settings and is the result
of many discussions and planning sessions about what the paraprofessional would need to know while working with the emotionally disturbed. Hayter provided the initiative for this project and was mainly responsible for Chapters 4, 7, and 8.
Shenkar provided many of the creative ideas behind the book
and was responsible for Chapters 1, 5, and 6. Beard provided
the stability and calming energy and was responsible for Chapters 2, 3, and 9. Chapter 10 was a joint effort.

The book is divided into two sections. Part I, entitled
"Theory, or Why It Happened," is intended to give the reader
a brief overview of the history and philosophy associated with
the treatment of the emotionally disturbed. This section is important because having a clear understanding of emotional disturbance leads to success in helping this group adjust to the
community. Part II, entitled "Practice, or How It Is Done,"
provides specific guidelines and treatment strategies for successfully helping the emotionally disturbed individual. The goal of
the book is to initiate the novice into working with the emotionally disturbed and to serve as a resource guide for the experienced practitioner.

A wise observation was once made regarding helping the
emotionally disturbed individual: "There are no bad patients,
only bad treatment plans." Our view is that no matter how
problematic, regressed, or unmotivated a person may seem to
be, change for the better is always possible. While we may
become frustrated if we expect to cure all of the problems that
we see, we can improve the quality of life of every person with
emotional problems. This may take the form of helping each
person build skills to overcome limitations or cope more effectively with stress. It may take the form of helping families or
friends learn more about a loved one's condition. It may simply
mean that we can educate the general public to understand that
the emotionally disturbed person is human and that this understanding in and of itself will improve the quality of life for the
emotionally disturbed.

As more individuals leave the state institutions and creative
community programs continue to emerge, there will be an in-

creasing demand for paraprofessionals. With the use of paraprofessionals, more personal attention can be given to individual
needs and problems. Group homes, day treatment programs,
crisis centers, and many other innovative programs are staffed
largely by paraprofessionals. While some mental health workers
hide in their offices and occasionally talk to individuals, the
paraprofessional works hours and days at a time, often with
some very disturbed individuals. With this in mind, we dedicate
this book to the paraprofessionals, the actual leaders in this new
movement of deinstitutionalization. The future of humane, innovative, and quality care lies in your hands.

We would like to thank the following people for their valu-
able comments, suggestions, and discussions, which have con-
tributed to the contents of this book: Fredrick Roberts, Paul
Chapman, Dion Taylor, Peter Facione, Jack Moss, Karen
Olthoff, Roger Facione, Barbara Nurenberg, Peggy Lawton,
Karen Spagnoli, Gretchen Rose, Janet Smade, Diane Lee,
Mark Lee, Tracy Markel, Karen Walter, Kristine Howard, Glo-
ria Smith, Connie Makowski, Roy Lewis, Diane Welsh, and
Dan Langowski.

ONE

Theory, or Why It Happened

1. *For Their Own Good*
A Historical Perspective

Historically, human beings have adapted to their environment in a manner reflecting the conditions of the time. We have struggled for centuries trying to improve our condition, the condition of our children, and the condition of human beings in general. Throughout history, our leaders have promised us peace and security and have created the rules needed to control and govern our lives. These rules were established "for our own good."

The deviant in society, that is the individual who acts, dresses, or behaves in a manner quite different from the majority of individuals, always has been a difficult individual to control. One such deviant in society is the individual who suffers from emotional disturbances, commonly called *mental illness*. In this chapter, we briefly outline society's treatment of the emotionally disturbed throughout history. It must be remembered that, although many of the treatments will seem unusually cruel and inhumane, such treatments actually were established to help individuals. They were treated in this manner "for their own good." However, "for their own good," in essence, is for society's good. Human beings generally prefer the status quo and often are frightened by change and by those who are different. The emotionally disturbed individual has suffered cruelty, tortures, and inhumane treatment for thousands of years. Even today, the less fortunate individual in society can be locked away for years in state institutions, tied up in physical restraints, and overmedicated to live a zombielike existence. It is quite possible that people in the future will be just as

17

amazed at how we "treated" the less fortunate in our society as we are by the treatments of the past.

BEFORE THE BEGINNING

Just as early man attributed storms, sickness, and bad harvests to the action of supernatural forces, so deviant behavior was explained as the result of possession by evil spirits. As early as 5000 years ago, a crude surgical technique called *trephining* was used as a rather direct way of dealing with these evil spirits. Trephining involved chipping a hole through the skull of the possessed person in order to allow the evil spirit to escape. Figure 1.1 demonstrates that some individuals actually survived this operation. This skull, found in Peru, shows evidence that the bone had time to heal before the individual died.

The idea that abnormal behavior was due to invasion by an evil spirit has endured for many centuries. References to possession can be found in the ancient records of the Chinese, the Egyptians, the Greeks, and the Hebrews. However, not all spirits were regarded as evil. A person could be invaded by a divine spirit as well, in which case the person's irrational utterances were regarded as divine truth. For example, in ancient Greece, the priestesses of the oracle of Apollo at Delphi would utter their replies in the mysterious language of the gods who were thought to inhabit their bodies. Such utterances were regarded as spoken by the divine spirit within.

The records that have survived, however, indicate that most possessions were considered invasions by evil spirits or the devil, which had to be drawn out of the person. This practice, called *exorcism,* involved a wide variety of techniques. Mild techniques could involve prayer, noisemaking, and the drinking of various potions. The more brutal techniques could involve submerging the possessed individual in water, whipping, and starvation in order to make the body a less comfortable habitation for the devil. Needless to say, many people died from such "cures." The death of the individual was attributed to the strength of the evil spirit rather than to the incompetence of the healer.

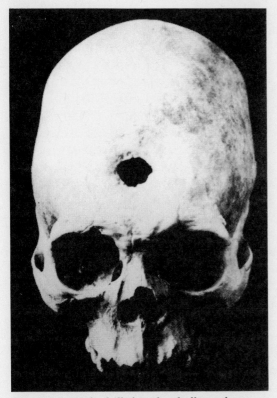

Figure 1.1. Hole drilled in the skull to release evil spirits. Courtesy of the Department of Library Services, American Museum of Natural History.

To many readers the ancient practice of exorcism appears crude, bizarre, and shockingly naive. However, even today, exorcisms reportedly still are performed by various religious groups, a fact brought to light by the popular horror movie, *The Exorcist.* In this film, an adolescent girl is possessed by the devil, who must be exorcised. The release of this motion picture led to a dramatic increase in individuals requesting exorcisms. Most Christian clergymen take a very dim view of exorcism, and cases of "possession" routinely are referred to psychiatrists (Calhoun, 1977).

Humane treatment of the emotionally disturbed began with

the ancient Greeks. The Greek physician Hippocrates (c. 460–c.360 B.C.) set about to prove that all illness, including "mental illness," was due to natural causes. His treatment methods were considerably more humane than those of the exorcistic tradition. Rest, music, exercise, diet, and other therapeutic activities were employed to help the disturbed individual.

With the fall of the Greek and Roman civilizations, this naturalistic psychology gave way to a resurgence of ancient superstition. Demonology was reborn in the Middle Ages. The emotionally disturbed individual once again was seen as possessed by the devil. During the Middle Ages, episodes of mass madness developed. For example, there are records indicating that bands of individuals roamed Europe ecstatically whipping themselves, or entire mobs would suddenly begin dancing frantically in the streets until they dropped from exhaustion. Numerous outbreaks of "dancing frenzy" were recorded throughout Europe. Elsewhere there were episodes of lycanthropy, in which individuals, particularly in rural villages, suddenly got the notion that they were wolves and began behaving as such. Our current legends about werewolves, vampires, and witches are based on actual events. Severely disturbed individuals often develop delusions that give them a sense of power and security. In a rural village in the Middle Ages, a wolf was a very powerful figure. Today Napoleon Bonaparte, a popular public figure, an alien from outer space, or a computerized robot are powerful figures. Human beings adapt to their environment in a manner reflecting the conditions of the time. We probably would find more computerized robots in our psychiatric hospitals today than werewolves, although it is quite probable that in the back wards of some of our larger state psychiatric hospitals we may still find a few werewolves, vampires, and witches.

Exorcisms again became very popular during the Middle Ages. The possessed were starved, dunked in hot water, chained, and flogged. One religious healer recorded the following prescription: "In case a man be lunatic, take a skin of mere-swine, work it into a whip, and swing (whip) the man forthwith; soon he will be well. Amen" (Zilboorg & Henry, 1941, p. 140). Another popular technique was to yell insults and violent curses at the possessed. The devil was known to be very proud, and it was hoped that the insults would hurt the devil's pride and drive him out of the possessed.

Early in the fifteenth century, the church distinguished between voluntary possession, in which the individual deliberately made a pact with the devil, and involuntary possession, in which the individual was possessed against his or her will. However, by the end of the fifteenth century, all persons who were severely disturbed were considered to be in voluntary possession by the devil, to be witches and sorcerers. Floods, poor weather, bad crops, miscarriages, or any distressing event was blamed on the individual in the village who was acting bizarrely. Since emotionally disturbed individuals frequently imagine that they have committed terrible sins or have engaged in exotic forbidden practices, it is not surprising to find that many of the accused freely confessed to whatever crimes they were charged with. When they did not confess freely, they were tortured until they did confess. Once the confession had been extracted, they were tried and killed.

Thus, the witch hunts began. It is estimated that from the middle of the fifteenth century to the end of the seventeenth, 100,000 people were executed as witches (Calhoun, 1977). Hunting down witches became a social and religious duty. Neighbors reported neighbors; everyone was suspect. Books and manuals explained how to recognize, examine, and sentence witches.

By the end of the seventeenth century, enlightened and influential people began to object to these gruesome and irrational practices. Thereafter, the treatment of the emotionally disturbed gradually entered a more rational phase. During this period hospitals for the emotionally disturbed had been founded in various cities. However, the dreadful conditions the emotionally disturbed endured in such "asylums" made the quick death of the witch-hunters seem almost merciful by comparison. The first mental hospital founded in Europe was the hospital of St. Mary at Bethlehem in London. This hospital, later called Bedlam, sold tickets so that the public could watch the patients howling in chains. In other hospitals, emotionally disturbed individuals were chained, caged, starved, preyed upon by rats, left for years lying naked in their own excrement, and as at Bedlam, displayed for the amusement of the public (Foucault, 1965). The first change in this system came in the late eighteenth century, through the work of Philippe Pinel (1745–1826), the chief physician at a large asylum in Paris during the French Revolution. It took the French Revolution to allow Pinel to introduce his "moral treatment."

MENTAL HEALTH'S THREE REVOLUTIONS

There have been three mental health revolutions. The first mental health revolution is identified with Philippe Pinel in France, William Tuke in England, and Benjamin Rush and Dorothea Dix in America. It was based on the notion that emotionally disturbed individuals should be treated with kindness and dignity. The second revolution was born in Vienna, in the work of Sigmund Freud. Freud directed attention to the intrapsychic life of people and emphasized the influence of unconscious conflicts on personality development. The third mental health revolution, while not identifiable with any one person, began in the 1950s with the introduction of psychotropic medications. Individuals who previously were hospitalized could be treated safely on an outpatient basis. Thus, community-based mental health services were born. Community Mental Health (CMH) was introduced in the 1960s. In the third revolution, public health concepts and strategies were applied to mental health services.

All three revolutions changed the public's assumptions about mental health and emotional disorders. Pinel's work led to the recognition that asylum inmates were "ill," not possessed by the devil. Freud taught that people are driven by forces over which they have no control, plagued as adults by the unresolved conflicts of childhood. The third revolution has shown that emotional problems are not the private misery of an individual but a social, ethical, and moral responsibility of the total community (Hobbs, 1964). The remainder of this chapter will emphasize the changes these revolutions have had on society. However, and most important, it will be emphasized that powerful as these revolutions have been, they have not been carried through successfully, and a fourth revolution is needed.

The beginnings of modern psychiatric theory and practice may be found in the innovations of Philippe Pinel in France. Pinel introduced what he and others called *moral treatment.* In the early nineteenth century, the notion of moral treatment for the emotionally disturbed certainly was a revolution. Patients in hospitals were unchained, their tortures ceased, and they began to be treated with humane and more rational methods.

Moral treatment meant psychological treatment; its principles were simple. The first principle was the elimination of cruelty. Physical force was to be used only to prevent the individual from hurting him- or herself or someone else, and not as punishment. Self-evident as this principle might seem, even today such a rule is difficult to enforce in many situations. Frightened staff members sometimes can be cruel. However, the introduction of tranquilizers helped ease fear on the part of personnel. With a technique of control that does not require physical intervention, the reassured staff is able more often to be kind and humane (Karon & Vandenbos, 1981).

The second principle was that if disturbed individuals could not be helped, then neither should they be subjected to harm, injury, humiliation, or contempt. The third principle of moral treatment was the keeping of accurate case records. From accurate histories, one could trace the origin of a problem and, thus, better help the individual.

The fourth principle was the importance of understanding that the disturbed persons were individual human beings. The emotionally disturbed were simply ordinary people with an extraordinary number of problems. Moral treatment aimed at restoring their emotional balance. This was accomplished, in part, by providing a pleasant and relaxed environment in which they could discuss their difficulties, live peacefully, and engage in some useful employment. More than anything else, moral treatment aimed at treating emotionally disturbed individuals like human beings. Records indicate that when moral treatment was the only treatment provided by mental hospitals in

Europe and America, at least 70 percent of those hospitalized for a year or less either improved or actually recovered.

The rise of mental hospitals in Europe and America followed closely upon the rise of cities. In the Middle Ages, the emotionally disturbed, along with other classes of dependents, were treated as a local responsibility, primarily within their own or other families. The growth of cities in the early nineteenth century changed the character of the problem, by increasing the concentration of the emotionally disturbed. There was a great demand for order and security, thus more mental hospitals were constructed and, by the 1840s, the psychiatric profession had begun. It has been suggested that the hospitals played a greater role in shaping psychiatry in the nineteenth century than psychiatry had played in shaping the hospitals (Starr, 1982).

The new hospitals were overcrowded almost immediately, thus dispelling the calm, tranquil atmosphere prescribed for moral treatment. These isolated hospitals also helped the public unlearn the lesson Pinel worked so hard to teach: that the emotionally disturbed were simply ordinary people. To the public, these huge hospitals seemed to conceal some dark horror and the emotionally disturbed once again were seen as freaks, dangerous and alien.

The second revolution in mental health occurred around the turn of the twentieth century, when Sigmund Freud (1856–1939) taught that the dark horrors were not behind the walls of mental hospitals but in people's minds. Through the development of the therapeutic techniques of psychodynamic theory, Freud treated individuals suffering from emotional disorders. Psychodynamic theory conceptualizes the human mind as an interaction of three forces: the id, the ego, and the superego. Each force has its own origin and its own specific role in maintaining normal personality functioning. Freud's psychodynamic theory indicated that people are driven by unconscious forces which affect how they behave and how their personalities develop.

Along with Darwin, Marx, and Einstein, Freud shaped our culture and beliefs about humanity in the twentieth century. His influence can be found in all sectors of contemporary life: novels, plays, poetry, television, movies, and even publications on infant and child care. However, his most important contribution to the field of mental health was in the utilization of psychodynamic theory in the treatment of the emotionally disturbed. Psychotherapy, a treatment that produces emotional and/or behavioral change in an individual, began to acquire wider public acceptance. By the 1930s and 1940s, therapists began reporting that even the most severely disturbed individuals could be helped with psychotherapy. The field of psychology expanded and the demand for psychotherapists increased. There is evidence to suggest that psychotherapy is a very effective tool in treating even the most severe emotional disturbances (Karon & Vandenbos, 1981).

The problem with psychotherapy was that it took too long. Severely disturbed individuals could be in therapy for years. In addition, many therapists did not have the patience to listen to the ravings of psychotics and preferred to treat the relatively quiet neurotics or slightly disturbed individuals in the comfort of their private offices. In order to deal with the severely disturbed individuals, two practices were developed: prefrontal lobotomy and electroconvulsive therapy (ECT). Prefrontal lobotomy, developed in 1935, is the surgical severing of the white matter tracts between the frontal lobes of the brain. Theoretically, aggressive, uncontrollable individuals would become calm and tranquil, enabling the severely disturbed to leave the mental hospitals after the operation. Thousands of these operations were performed before the procedure was abandoned. Unfortunately, many individuals emerged from surgery in a permanently vegetative state. Electroconvulsive therapy (ECT), also developed in the 1930s, involves administering to the individual an electric shock of approximately 70–130 volts, which induces a convulsion similar to a grand mal epileptic seizure. Although ECT still is used today, no one knows exactly how it works. Some say it "clears out" the nervous system, allowing it to return to normal functioning. Others say that the therapy is so aversive that the individual improves simply to avoid its repetition.

Through listening and counseling, psychotherapy helps an individual understand and resolve his or her emotional problems, always respecting the individual's right to be treated as a human being. Unfortunately, our understanding of the ways of human behavior is still in its infancy. Freud opened some doors, as have others, but much is still to be learned.

Mental health's third revolution began in the 1950s with the introduction of psychotropic medications. Psychotropic medications generally are tranquilizers and mood-stabilizing drugs, which help sedate the disturbed individual. The use of medication had dramatic effects. Violent, uncontrollable individuals could be calmed with tranquilizers. Other less hostile individuals showed marked improvement in the clarity of their thoughts and contact with reality. Some individuals improved so much that they no longer needed the structure of the mental hospital, and thus, the movement of deinstitutionalization began. However, an individual returning to the community after living in a hospital for 20 years might be expected to have difficulty functioning outside of the hospital. What was to be done?

The Kennedy Administration turned the cause of "community care" into a major federal program. In 1963, the Community Mental Health Centers Act was established to provide one mental health center for every 50,000 people. Anyone, rich or poor, who lived in the center's "catchment area" could use the center's psychological services. Furthermore, the centers were to implement programs for the prevention of emotional disturbance and to train professionals and paraprofessionals. Mental health's third revolution involved applying public health concepts (improving the community's well being) to mental health services. The individuals leaving the state hospitals were expected to receive the help they needed from the new community mental health centers.

Despite efforts to improve the state mental hospitals, many of them remained understaffed, dreary, and boring. Therefore, it is not surprising that, at present, the major efforts at improvement in mental health services are aimed at community mental health centers, which provide day treatment centers, group homes, work activity programs, aftercare programs, short-term inpatient services, emergency services, and other services to fill the needs of the community. Deinstitutionalization is the reality of today's mental health care system. A well-trained staff in the community mental health centers can provide more personal attention to the disturbed individual. The rationale of mental health's third revolution is that the emotionally disturbed can be served best in the least restrictive environment, which implies that the emotionally disturbed deserve as much freedom as possible. Some individuals may need a very structured and restrictive environment; however, most emotionally disturbed individuals do not require such restrictions. It is very possible that in the future there no longer will be large state mental hospitals, although smaller hospitals for severely disturbed individuals may still be needed.

Unfortunately, this third revolution has not been carried through successfully. Reports indicate that, at present, many emotionally disturbed individuals are homeless, wandering the streets aimlessly without adequate food, clothing, or shelter. A fourth revolution in mental health is necessary to finally bring peace to this disturbed population.

REVOLUTION FOUR AND BEYOND

Just as the first three revolutions in mental health, in one way or the other, changed the public's attitudes and feelings about the emotionally disturbed, a fourth revolution is needed in order to further this cause. The fourth revolution in mental health will call for the public acceptance of the emotionally disturbed. The emotionally disturbed will no longer wander the streets aimlessly, without adequate food, clothing, or shelter. Communities will no longer fear the opening of a group home for emotionally disturbed individuals in their neighborhoods. Those with emotional disturbances will seek help and no longer be embarrassed. The fourth revolution in mental health will confront the fear of the emotionally disturbed, a fear based on a wish never to see ourselves like "them," a fear of those regions of the mind that still haunt us.

The future of mental health can take many directions. The community mental health program may be replaced by corporate mental health programs. Already, in the medical field, private corporations have taken over many aspects of health care; several major corporations own and operate a large percentage of hospitals in America. It is very possible that this trend also will be carried over to the field of mental health. Many group homes and small psychiatric hospitals already are corporate owned.

In the future, we hope to see more preventative measures in the mental health field. This may include better education on prenatal care, more infant studies, and a general emphasis on health. Already, there are child guidance and infant care centers. Parenting classes, economic aid, education, and a higher standard of living all are excellent prevention measures. The early detection and prevention of emotional disorders should be given primary attention.

We also see an expansion in the field of neuropsychology and the continued growth of insights into the workings of the human mind. Psychotropic medications could be refined with attention to action on specific brain centers and fewer side effects. In addition, the continued advancements in computer technology will have a major bearing on the field.

Individuals will no longer spend their lives in state institutions; this already is a thing of the past. Community placement of the emotionally disturbed will grow with community acceptance. Community acceptance will grow with community education offered through the schools and the media. Paraprofessionals will be needed in increasing numbers. Psychotherapy and various environmental therapies will be refined and utilized with excellent results. The field of mental health will be looked upon not as a mysterious and somewhat odd field but as a powerful profession at the forefront of progressive change.

The history of the treatment of the emotionally disturbed individual in society is a fascinating yet sad story. It seems incredible that only a few hundred years ago such individuals were tortured. In this chapter, some of the more outstanding features of this history have been traced, emphasizing the three revolutions in mental health.

The first revolution was led by Philippe Pinel, the second revolution by Sigmund Freud, and the third revolution by the concept of community mental health. All three revolutions were aimed at changing public attitudes about the emotionally disturbed. However, these revolutions were not completely successful, and a fourth revolution is needed. The fourth revolution will bring about public acceptance, which will come gradually through continued community placement, public education, and further knowledge about the field. Today we tend to treat labels: *mental illness, paranoid schizophrenia, manic-depression.* A human being is more than a psychiatric label and deserves to be helped in a kind, dignified, respectful manner.

2. *What Is Your Sign?*
Diagnosis

The bar was dark. The music was loud. Bruce walked into the room and surveyed all the women—strangers. He boldly approached a slender brunette at the counter and uttered his usual line.

"Hiya, what's your sign?"

"Buzz off," she replied.

He moved on, knowing it was only a matter of time before his charm and wit would yield a more favorable outcome.

"What's your sign?" Bruce continued, until four other women in the place had rejected his advances.

In the corner sat Debbie. She frequented this place a lot. She usually sat in the same corner, always alone. Bruce spied Debbie and thought to himself, "Boy, that one is really a loser." He sat down next to her and began speaking. "Hey, what's your sign?"

Debbie was startled and looked up. "Huh?" she replied.

"I said, what's your sign?" Bruce continued.

"Oh I'm a schizophrenic," Debbie said.

"Oh right, that's mid-September through mid-October?" Bruce replied cooly.

"No, no," Debbie stated, "my shrink told me I'm a schizophrenic."

"You mean crazy?" Bruce felt a little uncomfortable and decided to leave. As he turned, he left Debbie with one final comment. "Yea, I'm crazy too, but at least I'm normal. You're really weird."

The terms *crazy, insane, nuts, mad, lunatic,* or *mentally ill* all

are common ways of describing people who are somehow not
"normal" to the rest of us. Like most generalizations, these
labels say very little about the person so labeled, nor do they
help anybody understand what a person is going through. So,
just as a person is much more than only a zodiac sign, a person
suffering with emotional disturbance is much more than the
label or diagnosis given to them.

Diagnose means to determine what a problem is. Your car
undergoes a diagnostic tune-up to pinpoint any engine difficulty for proper repair. Or, a doctor might diagnose a fractured
ankle from X rays and the great pain you feel in your lower leg
after you slip on a wet floor. Most people feel they understand
a problem better when it is given a name. Once a diagnosis is
given, that is, once the problem is determined, steps usually are
taken to fix whatever is wrong. Unfortunately, diagnosing emotional disturbances does not follow in such a straightforward
manner. True, there are extensive systems for naming emotional problems, but this does not lead to exact procedures for
curing those problems. In fact, sometimes diagnostic labels can
lock people into stereotyped categories. These labels may
block people from receiving what they might need the most.

An engine diagnosed as having fouled plugs needs a new set
of spark plugs. A broken ankle needs to be set in a cast. But a
diagnosis of schizophrenia neither explains what is wrong nor
points out how the difficulty should be handled. In the area of
emotional problems, diagnosis is a shorthand method of commu-
nicating what is happening within a certain person. From this
beginning, goals for treatment can be set. Treatment of emotional disturbance concentrates on understanding and changing
the problem issues.

Despite the limits on diagnosis, anyone working with the
emotionally disturbed will need to be familiar with the various
types of diagnostic categories. This chapter will present an overview of five areas of emotional disturbance: neurotic disorders,
psychosomatic disorders, personality disorders, organic brain
disorders, and psychotic disorders. This overview is intended to
help practitioners understand the diagnoses given the clients
they help treat; it is not intended as a guideline for *making*
diagnoses.

NEUROTIC DISORDERS

Somewhere between normal behavior and severe disturbance lie the problems called *neuroses* or *neurotic disorders*.
Everyone faces day-to-day stress, pressure, and frustration,
and copes in ways they have found to work best. These challenges are needed to encourage people to change their lives
and to make life rewarding and worthwhile. But sometimes,
how people cope with life does not work out in satisfactory
ways, and leaves them feeling uncomfortable and out of control
of the situation. The threatening feeling of not being in control
is given a label, such as *anxiety, conflict,* or *distress*. People who
cannot successfully manage these threatening feelings are likely
to feel more anxiety and distress; then the situation is termed a
neurotic disorder. More simply, a neurosis is present when anxieties begin to interfere with a person's daily functioning and
behavior.

Michael suffers from a debilitating disorder, agoraphobia,
generally known as a fear of open spaces. Michael's case is particularly severe because he also is troubled by accompanying
panic attacks. Michael has not left the confines of his apartment
for periods of up to six months at a time. He has left only for
infrequent doctor's appointments. Otherwise, he arranges to
meet all his needs either by deliveries or by visits from his few
remaining friends. He is unable to work or socialize outside his
apartment. Every occasion has to be forfeited, since whenever
he leaves the safety of his home he begins to feel uncomfortable
and experiences difficulty breathing. Michael describes his experience in this way: "I get the feeling that I'm choking to death,
that I can't get to safety." Michael has been hospitalized in
several emergency rooms after experiencing one of his panic
attacks.

Michael suffers from a neurotic disorder. People attempt to
cope with life's problems in many other unsuccessful ways. All
individuals react differently to the anxieties or pressures they
experience. The various ways in which people unsuccessfully
manage anxiety is the basis for labeling the types of neurotic
disorders.

Remember, a diagnosis is a shorthand method of stating

groups of symptoms or problems. Symptoms are a particular person's unsuccessful or excessive attempts to cope with anxiety. Table 2.1 lists many of the common neurotic disorders and their symptoms. People may not be aware of their neuroses, sensing only that things are not going as well as they should. However, neurotic problems are rarely solved by digging in and trying to do better. Successful resolution of the problems may require outside professional help or at least some wise self-help suggestions.

On the other hand, the little quirks and corners of personalities may not greatly impair people's lives; they learn to live with them. To some extent, nearly everyone experiences phobias, which are irrational fears of some thing. Table 2.2 lists many of the more common varieties.

PSYCHOSOMATIC DISORDERS

"I'm so upset. I just had an awful day. My head aches, my stomach is churning, and I feel so jittery," Thelma complained to George, her husband.

"Oh settle down. You'll be fine. Your troubles are all in your head," George answered. He, too, had had a difficult day.

"Maybe you're right. I shouldn't let things bother me so much," Thelma agreed.

"That's right. You'll give yourself an ulcer if you keep letting your emotions get the best of you. Just relax and take it easy, like I do. It's mind over matter," George encouraged, automatically.

"You are right! I feel better already. By the way, remember that telephone pole by the school? I knocked it over with the car today, minor damage. I was really upset but your reasoning has helped me to take things more philosophically," Thelma beamed.

"What!?!"

This exchange illustrates what we all know, events can influence feelings. Emotions can affect physical being. Psychosomatic disorders are physical symptoms brought on by emotions and stress. It could be said that the problem originates "in one's

Table 2.1
COMMON NEUROTIC DISORDERS

Disorder	Symptoms
Depression	Sadness, "the blues," usually brought on by some type of loss from which the person cannot bounce back. Often accompanied by problems in appetite, sleeping, or concentrating. The person often is irritable or has feelings of hopelessness for the future. Similar to normal mourning.
Phobia	Intense fear or dread of an object or situation. Panic is out of proportion to actual physical danger (see Table 2.2).
Hypochondria	Imagined problems of health; excessive worry over coming down with some illness or disease; preoccupation with functioning of the body.
Obsession Compulsion	Constant and unwelcome thoughts that cannot be stopped (obsessions); strong impulses to act on thoughts, often over and over again (compulsions); overattention to insignificant details.
Neurasthenia	Constant weakness, fatigue, and lack of energy; the capacity to laugh and enjoy is diminished or lost.
Hysteria: Conversion Type	Anxiety converted into physical symptoms; the body's senses are impaired with no physical cause; loss of sight, hearing, or touch due to emotional problems.
Hysteria: Disassociation	Loss of awareness and consciousness of ongoing activity; sleepwalking, amnesia, or in more severe cases, split and multiple personalities.

Table 2.2
COMMON PHOBIAS

Fear	Phobia
High places	Acrophobia
Crowds or open spaces	Agoraphobia
Pain	Algophobia
Thunder and/or lightning	Astra- and/or astrapophobia
Closed in places	Claustrophobia
Work	Ergasiophobia
Crossing a bridge	Gephyrophobia
Marriage	Gamophobia
Blood	Hematophobia
Water	Hydrophobia
Being alone	Monophobia
Guns	Mypaphobia
Darkness	Nyctophobia
Disease	Pathophobia
Public speaking	Phonophobia
Death	Thanatophobia
Strangers	Xenophobia
Animals	Zoophobia

head," but the results are present and real. This differs significantly from hysteria or hypochondria, where actual tissue damage is absent. If the stress or emotions are not reduced or rechanneled, psychosomatic disorders can cause physical symptoms that frequently will need medical attention. Problems can range from mild, such as an upset stomach, to severe, as in a peptic ulcer. As stated earlier, all people have stress. The difference is whether the stress can be dealt with positively or negatively. If the stressful situation cannot be handled positively, the result often will show up in symptoms. If the symptoms include actual tissue damage, the problem is called *psychosomatic*. Of course, not all medical difficulties are stress related. However, many physical difficulties are known to be caused or made worse by psychological reactions to stress. Table 2.3 includes some of the difficulties related to stress.

Table 2.3
BODILY EXPRESSIONS OF STRESS

Body System	Type of Ailment
Musculoskeletal	Backache
	Arthritis
	Tension headache
Respiratory	Asthma
	Hiccoughs
	Hyperventilation
Cardiovascular	Migraine headache
	Hypertension (high blood pressure)
Skin	Eczema
	Acne
	Hives
Gastrointestinal	Ulcers
	Constipation
	Diarrhea
	Heartburn
	Gastritis
Genitourinary	Dysmenorrhea
	Impotence

Remember in psychosomatic disorders the symptom is physical but psychological factors play a large part in causation. Other problems not listed in the table but often considered to have psychological components include insomnia, certain allergies, anorexia nervosa, and bulimia.

It is particularly noteworthy to consider that even positive events can add to the strain of life. Table 2.4 indicates how stress builds up from all types of sources. The scale developed by Holmes and Rahe points out that just about anyone can develop stress-related problems.

Table 2.4
THE SOCIAL READJUSTMENT SCALE

Rank	Life Event	Mean Value
1	Death of a spouse	100
2	Divorce	73
3	Marital separation	65
4	Jail term	63
5	Death of a close family member	63
6	Personal injury or illness	63
7	Marriage	50
8	Fired at work	47
9	Marital reconciliation	45
10	Retirement	45
11	Change in health of family member	44
12	Pregnancy	40
13	Sex difficulties	39
14	Gain of new family member	39
15	Business readjustment	39
16	Change in financial status	38
17	Death of a close friend	37
18	Change to new line of work	36
19	Change in number of arguments with spouse	35
20	Mortgage over $10,000	31
21	Foreclosure on mortgage or loan	30
22	Change in work responsibilities	29
23	Son or daughter leaving home	29
24	Trouble with in-laws	29
25	Outstanding personal achievement	28
26	Wife begins or stops work	26
27	Begin or end of school	26
28	Change in living conditions	25
29	Revision of personal habits	24
30	Trouble with boss	23
31	Change in work hours or condition	20
32	Change in residence	20
33	Change in schools	20
34	Change in recreation	19
35	Change in church activities	19
36	Change in social activities	18
37	Mortgage or loan less than $10,000	17
38	Change in sleeping habits	16
39	Change in number of family get togethers	15

40	Change in eating habits	15
41	Vacation	13
42	Christmas	12
43	Minor violation of the law	11

Note: Circle any of the life events above you have experienced in the past twelve months. Total the points assigned to each event (mean value column) and compare your score to the risk categories. Categories of risk: 300+ = High risk of major illness or injury; 150–300 = Moderate risk of major illness or injury; and under 150 = Low risk of major illness or injury.

Source: From "The Social Readjustment Scale" by T. H. Holmes and R. H. Rahe. *Journal of Psychosomatic Research* 11, no. 2 (1967), 213–218.

PERSONALITY DISORDERS

The adult personality is made up of many patterns of behavior. Each person has a unique way of relating to others and to the environment in general. A personality disorder is a deeply ingrained, habitual pattern of acting that is maladaptive in some way. Maladaptive means that one's way of relating to others is based solely on meeting one's own needs at the expense of others. This leads to a significant disruption of interpersonal relations. In general, what sets apart a personality disorder from, say, "stubbornness" is that interpersonal relationships are continually disrupted. If a person does not develop successful relationships with anyone, the possibility of a personality disorder is a diagnostic consideration. A developing pattern of personality disorder frequently is seen while the person is still an adolescent. The problematic pattern continues through most of the adult life. It is noteworthy that the pattern does tend to subside or become less evident in mid-life or older age, but the overall style of relating usually is lifelong.

There are many types of personality disorders. Table 2.5 lists those most likely to be encountered by the practitioner. Perhaps the most well-known category of personality disorder is the "antisocial" personality. This classification includes those who display repeated criminal behavior, chronic substance abuse, or ongoing sexual deviancy. The key element in the antisocial personality is the complete lack of feeling for the rights and welfare of others and a disregard for the rules of the

Table 2.5
TYPES OF PERSONALITY DISORDERS

Disorder	Symptoms
Antisocial	Disregard for social obligations or laws (chronic criminal behavior or truancy); little or no feeling for the welfare of others; poor impulse control (frequent fighting or vandalism); ongoing sexual deviancy (prostitution or promiscuity); consistent failure to meet obligations.
Borderline	Instability in areas of relationships, behavior, mood, and self-image; unable to form long-term goals or commitments; low toleration for being alone; chronically bored with life; unpredictable.
Dependent/ Inadequate	Allows or maneuvers others into assuming responsibility for the inadequate person's life; weak response to everyday life; unable to make decisions; little self-confidence.
Explosive	Unstable and aggressive; frequent blowups by a person who is not unsocial otherwise; outbursts of anger, hate, violence, or affection.
Histrionic/ Hysterical	Overly dramatic; intense overreactions; craves attention; may be seen as charming at first but eventually perceived by others as vain and demanding.
Narcissistic	Self-absorbed; overly involved with own feelings; overvalues own ability; exhibitionist or sets unrealistic goals.
Passive/ Aggressive	Aggression shown in passive or hidden manner such as pouting, procrastination, stubbornness, or intentional mistakes or foul ups; purposely forgetful; behavior continues even if more effective behavior is within ability.
Schizoid	Withdrawn, emotionally aloof, and cool; few friends; often seen as eccentric or odd; avoids social interaction.

society. Antisocial personalities frequently come to the attention of mental health systems by way of the criminal justice system. As you might imagine, there is often debate over whether people with antisocial personalities are really emotionally disturbed. Whatever your philosophical stance may be, it is clear that the antisocial personality is different from the norm and people with such disorders are problems to society.

Since, by definition, the personality disorder includes deeply ingrained patterns that often begin in childhood, it should not come as a surprise that personality disorders are difficult to change. In part this is because the individuals diagnosed as having personality disorders usually do not see their own behavior as being dysfunctional. However, others around them experience the personality disorder as undesirable. Treatment of individuals diagnosed as having personality disorders focuses on getting them to develop more socially acceptable ways of getting their needs met.

ORGANIC BRAIN DISORDERS

While working with the emotionally disturbed, sooner or later you will encounter a person with problems referred to as *organic*. This is a catch-all phrase to describe problems that result from some type of physical damage to the brain. More formal terms for brain damage are *dementia, delirium,* and *senility*. The damage may prevent the brain from developing normally or continuing at the previous level of functioning. It is important to differentiate organic brain disorders from psychosomatic disorders. Both involve actual damage to the body. The difference is that, with psychosomatic disorders, the psychological problem is the origin of the physical disorder. With organic brain disorders, the tissue damage to the brain is the basis of any resulting behavioral or psychological difficulty. The changes in the brain, or the physical problem, is the origin of the psychological or behavioral disorder. Behavioral changes often seen in organic problems include confusion, loss of memory, easy irritability, low tolerance for change, and hallucinations. Other serious damage can result in the loss of speech, vision, hearing, or mobility. If damaged areas of the brain involve basic life sup-

Table 2.6
POTENTIAL CAUSES OF ORGANIC BRAIN SYNDROME (OBS)

Cause	Description
Infection	Inflammation of the brain (encephalitis), or transmitted disease (e.g., syphilis, acquired immune deficiency syndrome [AIDS])
Trauma (blow to the head)	Concussion: brief loss of consciousness due to jarring of the brain; contusion, coma, or convulsions due to the brain being shifted out of position; laceration: foreign object cuts or damages brain tissue
Vascular interference	Stroke: blood clot stops flow of blood to the brain; hemorrhage: broken blood vessels result in bleeding in the brain; tumor: abnormal growth of brain cells
Tissue degeneration	Senility or Alzheimer's disease: decay of brain tissue resulting in deterioration of control of emotions, intellect, and motor functioning
Lack of nutrition	Lack of niacin (pellagra); lack of B1 (beriberi); shortage of vitamins related to alcoholic intake or lifestyle (Korsakoff's syndrome)
Ingesting of toxins: Drug overdose Alcohol Carbon monoxide Mushrooms Lead and other heavy metals (e.g., mercury)	Organic symptoms vary according to toxin

port, loss of consciousness or even death can result. Organic problems are often seen in aging people; however, organicity is associated with many different causes. Advancing age, by itself, is not a cause for brain damage; there always is another factor. Table 2.6 lists many sources of organic brain problems.

Other diagnoses, such as epilepsy and mental retardation, sometimes are included in discussions of organic brain disorders. Even a brief consideration of these areas is outside the scope of this chapter. See Evans (1983) or Svoboda (1979) in the reference section for additional information on these subjects.

PSYCHOTIC DISORDERS

Of all the problems that face human beings, the difficulties labeled as *psychoses* are among the most troubling. People with psychotic disorders present an unexpected picture. Frequently, they look no different than anybody else; often between episodes of disturbance they may act in relatively normal ways. But the internal conflict and confusion experienced by those suffering with psychosis is major and devastating.

Psychosis is disruption of all the things that make human beings unique. Thought, emotion, and interpersonal behavior can all be distorted. Because of the intensity of the problems, psychotic persons are pushed further and further away from what they need most, successful human contact.

In the continuum of emotional disturbances, psychosis is the most severe. The problems experienced are the furthest from normal. While neuroses and psychosomatic disorders are troublesome, the emotional pain and suffering of the psychotic individual seems to be multiplied a hundred times. The pain and upset of family and friends also is magnified.

There are two major classifications of psychotic disorders: affective disorders and schizophrenic disorders.

Affective Disorders

Affect refers to mood. Mood can be high or low or anywhere in between. Everyone experiences changes in mood depending on what is happening. Mood swings that go too far up or too far down present a problem; moods that shift rapidly also can cause great difficulty. Table 2.7 reviews affective disorders. The psychotically depressed person shows many of the same symptoms seen in neurotic depression. That is, there may be loss of appetite, difficulty sleeping, and loss of interest in

Table 2.7
THE AFFECTIVE DISORDERS

Disorder	Symptoms
Psychotic depression	Severe low mood; loss of interest in all usual activity; intense guilt feelings and the experience of being worthless or unworthy of life; serious suicide risk. Events that cause the problems are difficult to pinpoint; a possible cause may be biological or chemical in nature.
Mania	Euphoric mood; hyperactive behavior with thoughts racing and rapid speech pattern; high self-opinion; decreased sleep; easily distracted with difficulty concentrating.
Manic/depression	A shifting from one extreme mood to the other; true syndrome occurs in a regular pattern; few actual cases.

previously pleasurable activities. The differences lie in part in the severity of the problem, which is far greater in psychosis. The psychotically depressed person typically will exhibit intense guilt over real or imagined mistakes or sins, perhaps to the point of losing touch with reality and focusing solely on the guilt and need for punishment. A psychotically depressed person may have extreme thoughts like, "I am no good to the human race and should be killed," or "My insides have been rotted out because of my sins." A major worry of those dealing with the psychotically depressed is the possibility of suicide, as it would be in dealing with a severely depressed neurotic person. Often, the person may feel that his or her hopeless or unworthy condition cannot be solved in any other way.

Many researchers feel that there is a distinct difference other than severity alone between neurotic and psychotic depression. The theory is that neurotic depression is always brought on by some type of loss. It is mourning that has not yet been worked out. Psychotic depression is thought to be related more to biochemistry and less to environmental influences. Psychotic depression is believed to occur in ongoing patterns or cycles. The differences do have some relevance as to how the problems are treated.

Unusually elevated moods are called *manic* or *mania*. People experiencing this disorder display a seemingly limitless supply of energy and ideas. The problem is that the ideas come too fast and the resulting behavior accomplishes few successful results. Many projects may be begun, but the racing thoughts preclude the time to complete anything before the person is thinking about the next project. During a manic episode, the person's speech usually is loud and rapid; the person seems to be unable to get out all there is to say. Sleep is decreased. Self-esteem is inflated. In general, manic people may feel that they can do anything about everything. They rarely are aware of the demands they place on themselves or others. Problems develop as the body, inevitably, becomes exhausted from such feverish activity. There also is the danger of injury from attempting dangerous stunts as a result of their distorted thinking.

Some people experience both depression and mania, a psychosis known as *manic-depression* or *bipolar disorder*. In this disorder, the mood swings from one extreme to the other in a more or less regular pattern. Actually, true cases of regular patterned bipolar shifts, from depression to mania to depression, are rare.

In the acute (most severe) phase of either depression or mania, hospitalization is needed to provide both physical safety and the emotional stability of outside control. In severe chronic depression, when other treatment strategies have failed, sometimes electroconvulsive therapy (ECT) may be administered. This is done to help break the depressive thought patterns that the person cannot stop alone.

Schizophrenic Disorders

In the United States today, over 2 million Americans—that is, one person out of a hundred—suffer from the disorder called *schizophrenia*. Schizophrenia is a complex mix of problems that devastate the entire personality with distortions in thinking, emotions, and behavior. For now, we will simply describe the symptoms of schizophrenia. Later chapters will explore how symptoms develop and why the schizophrenic person uses these unusual ways of coping with life.

To begin with, the thinking process is affected in ways that lead the person to misinterpret what is really happening. The schizophrenic may experience delusions, hallucinations, false ideas of reference, blocking, or withdrawal. Each of these problems will be described.

Delusions are false beliefs that are maintained even though facts and reality dispute the belief. One person told us that his brain had been removed while he was asleep. He claimed that scientists studied his brain and then replaced it with a brain from another person. When we countered with the improbability of such an operation, he explained that the CIA had advanced surgical procedures that the general public and regular physicians did not know about. As is frequently the case with delusional thinking, the person could not be talked out of his belief by facts alone.

Hallucinations are false perceptions by the senses when no outside stimulation is present. Hearing voices is the most common phenomenon reported. The next most frequent is visual distortions, or seeing things that are not really there. Others will report odd odors or body disturbances. Hallucinations usually provoke strong anxiety or fear. One person was troubled by a woman's voice telling him to jump off the bus whenever he rode one. Another said that the television told her to destroy all the computers in the world. Besides the distress the hallucinations themselves create, the problem may be even more dangerous if the person cannot resist what he or she "hears" or experiences.

False ideas of reference are feelings that all events or all people somehow affect you. Such feelings may be pleasurable. One man believed he had discovered the cure for cancer in the "oil of skunks." Therefore, he felt all the money in the universe should be paid to him for this great contribution. Such feelings of reference can also be unpleasant. One woman found it difficult to relax. She constantly watched those around her. She believed that anyone who laughed or smiled was making fun of her or thinking bad thoughts about her. It is difficult to work with those who are so self-absorbed that they find it hard to think about anything but themselves and how others must be against them.

Blocking refers to gaps in the thinking process. Usually a person's thoughts and speech flow logically from one idea to the next. The schizophrenic, however, often seems to have pieces missing in the uptake and outflow of information. Speech may be confusing to others because key parts are left out or implied by symbols. Unfortunately, no one else understands the symbols; therefore, blocking stops communication. Following is an example of schizophrenic thought patterns as reflected in writing. The words themselves are understandable but the whole thought is very confusing:

THE USE OF STEERING KNOBS by Martin D.

The use of steering knobs shouldn't be considered on little children's kiddy cars but should be considered on all Fords, Buicks, Oldsmobiles, Toyotas, Chevrolets, GMC Trucks, Pontiacs, Volkswagens, Datsuns, Dodges, Plymouth vans and autos, BMW's, Audis, Whites, Diamond Roes, Deutzs and all blue '71–'75 Ford pick-up trucks.

On Sunday May 15th in the year of our Lord nineteen hundred and eighty three, about the fourteen-hundredth hour of the day it was merely a fact that motor-cycles don't need them, but on the other hand is a ring and on the left a clutch. This fact I consider irrelevant and the reason for all this conjecture, when I was riding down Main Street on the sidewalk also on my bike a blue late model Ford pick-up who also like me wanted a cigarette pulled in front of me and revved his engine. I had a sound gut feeling and he whipped in slowly because he didn't have a steering knob.

Withdrawal refers to the tendency to retreat into one's own world of thoughts and fantasies. Normal interaction with others depends on separating wishes from what actually happens in the real world. Withdrawal can be extreme enough that one rejects reality in favor of one's wish of what reality should be. One person spent hours looking in mirrors at himself. When asked why he did this his response was, "I'm the only one who understands me."

The second area of disturbance in schizophrenia is emotions. More than any other way, people interact with each other through their feelings. The schizophrenic person experiences many confusing and frightening feelings; unusual thoughts and behavior frequently are a result of distorted feelings. Typically seen as a symptom in schizophrenia is "inappropriate" affect. This refers to the expression of emotion that does not match with how a person normally would be expected to react. In one example, a therapy group was discussing milestones in their lives. Most of the tales were sad and this led others in the group to tell of sad things that had happened to them. One woman related a tale of how she had found a dead body floating in a river. The group members expected this to be sad, or at least unpleasant. Instead the woman had on an ear-to-ear grin, stating, "it was great," as she proceeded to describe the corpse.

Other people may show a certain lack or blunting of emotion. This is frequently termed *flat affect*. In reality, this is a case of overcontrol of emotion as opposed to lack of feeling. Persons suffering with schizophrenia experience many feelings. Unfortunately, they experience most outside contact as frightening. This fear lies at the heart of much of the schizophrenic symptomatology. Actually, fear is too soft a description—the emotion experienced is panic. They panic over relationships. They panic over intimacy. Yet, they also fear the pervasive feelings of isolation and aloneness. Figure 2.1 gives some idea about the emotional turmoil of the schizophrenic person.

The third area of disturbance in schizophrenia is behavior. People labeled as schizophrenic often display all sorts of unusual behavior. This may include odd, idiosyncratic things (for example, one person was directing traffic totally naked) or bizarre, seemingly intolerable situations (for example, a girl burned herself with lit cigarettes to "let me know I'm still here and alive"). As difficult as it may be to figure out, all this behavior has meaning to the schizophrenic person. Others around may find it difficult or impossible to figure out, but all behavior has meaning. The emotionally disturbed individual's odd behavior certainly stands out, and in the past, the stereo-

*Figure 2.1. Self-portrait by a schizophrenic
person.*

typical behavior of schizophrenics led to labeling them *lunatics*
and confining them to strait jackets. The behavior of the schizophrenic is designed to keep others away, either physically or
emotionally. This compelling need will be explored more fully
in Chapter 3.

The various difficulties of schizophrenia tend to cluster into
symptom patterns. These groupings of symptoms form the basis for different types or categories of schizophrenia. Table 2.8
lists various kinds of schizophrenia frequently designated.

The previous section concentrated on the symptoms associated with schizophrenia. The following section will present a
different, possibly more helpful way to look at the types of
schizophrenia. Christian Beels, a psychiatrist, has described the

Table 2.8
THE SCHIZOPHRENIC DISORDERS

Disorder	Symptoms
Paranoid	Most common form of the disturbance. The person experiences delusions either of being important ("I am Jesus Christ") or of being persecuted by others ("The FBI is bugging my room"); tends to be highly suspicious and feels there is some type of plot against him or her or that someone is trying to control his or her thoughts and actions; may experience hallucinations, such as voices that accuse or prod. Sufferers often are of average or above-average intelligence levels.
Catatonic	Motor activity is most dramatic, either rigid and immobile or excited and hyperactive; during withdrawn phase person may be so far from reality that he or she can stay in the same position for hours or rock for long periods and refuse food and drink; during excited phase person may display wild activity, injure self or others, and need help controlling actions.
Disorganized	Speech, thinking, and behavior are incoherent or childlike; strange gestures and odd facial expressions are common; mood is silly and responses to others may be blank stares or a stream of giggling. This form was once known as hebephrenia.
Chronic undifferentiated	The person may display various symptoms of the other types but with much less sharpness; mood is usually flat or blunted; stress may cause symptoms to become more intense; hygiene and interpersonal skills are lacking or decline.

long-term development of schizophrenia in terms of *careers in schizophrenia*. These careers may be acute, periodic, or chronic. The focus here is on the changes over time that the person suffering from schizophrenia experiences and the problems that arise. The different careers will be explored by describing three people. Each has been diagnosed as schizophrenic, but each manifests symptoms differently. To be successful in working with each schizophrenic, workers need to understand the differences and what is happening to the person during his or her "career."

CAREERS IN SCHIZOPHRENIA

Acute Schizophrenia

Don was 24 years old when he experienced his "nervous breakdown." His family took him to the emergency room of a local hospital after he had ransacked his own home and killed the family cat. Don's reason for his action was that the cat was sending him messages and needed to be stopped. Don's mother explained to the emergency room nurse that the problem happened all of a sudden, and nobody knew that Don was having difficulty. However, during later discussions with a psychiatrist, it became more apparent to Don and his family that even though this acute episode seemingly had happened "out of the blue," Don had been experiencing trouble for some time. Prior to the blow up, he had become quieter and more of a loner. He and his girlfriend were not getting along; in fact, the relationship had ended some weeks earlier. Also, Don lost his job four months prior to the incident. At the time, Don said he had been laid off; now he admitted that he had been fired. Don was fired following an argument with his supervisor during which he accused the company of bugging his delivery truck. Don believed they were spying on him.

The concept of a career points up the duration of the problem. Acute problems can last a few hours or up to six months. A "nervous breakdown" or schizophrenic episode happens when a person's ability to cope with life has been exhausted. As stated previously, all behavior has meaning, and the extraordinary behavior during a schizophrenic episode has meaning, too. Others may see the behavior as bizarre, but those experiencing the problems are only trying to cope with difficulties they are not emotionally equipped to handle. Typically, first episodes are seen between the ages of 16 and 25. It is no coincidence that this is the time in life when the individual is attempting to become an adult. Simply stated, the acute schizophrenic break reflects the inability of an individual to properly adjust to being an adult in the adult world. Schizophrenic symptoms are ways of coping with changes; they are failed attempts to cope with stress. They can also be seen as attempts to retreat from or push away the unpleasant experiences of life. At first, Don refused to acknowledge that anything was wrong, even though his problems had cost him both his job and his girlfriend within a short period of time. This is a common reaction. But unless there is some type of intervention, the problems wili continue to mount despite the denials. Typically, the schizophrenic person will respond to thoughts, feelings, or stress in some way that forces others to intervene. In Don's case, his family insisted that he go to the hospital. Even in the face of destroyed belongings and the slain family pet, Don denied that anything was wrong. He only agreed to go to the hospital when his brother suggested he needed a rest.

In every case of an acute schizophrenic episode, there has been a buildup of stress. Additionally, there always is some event that triggers the acute episode, the proverbial straw that breaks the camel's back. The event and the trauma surrounding it may be clear to anyone who has the facts. That is, it is easy to understand the significance of a sudden accident or major loss. More often, though, the precipitating event is apparently minor, and others cannot understand easily why a seemingly small event could be so devastating to someone else. In many cases, the actual causes or deep roots of the problem will never be determined without long, in-depth investigation by a highly trained therapist. Nonetheless, the paraprofessional can be of assistance in an acute crisis situation.

The acute or crisis period is very important in treatment because the person and significant others around him or her are most in need of solutions and most open to direction and change.

It is important that assistance be obtained and the problems explored. Some people do recover without intervention, but without some type of exploration, change is unlikely—and without change, the same problems are likely to recur.

During the acute phase of schizophrenia, treatment must focus on building skills to cope and providing reassurance that the person is safe and will not be harmed. Verbal interaction, medication, and inpatient care are the most common forms of treatment. Medication helps the individual cope with intense anxiety. The inpatient unit provides external structure and security that are felt to be lost internally by the individual. Talking provides human interaction, assuring the person that he or she is not all alone in the struggle against fear and confusion. Perhaps the break even can be seen as a potentially positive reaction, if the person can accept that this is an opportunity to understand what has happened and learn and grow from it.

Periodic Schizophrenia

Martin is a 26-year-old construction worker. When he works, he is paid well, but the work is seasonal. Martin attended a junior college but was never able to complete a full year of class. He went into the hospital every six to eight months because of psychotic thinking and behavior. When doing well, Martin is outgoing, talkative, and pleasant to be around. However, when his stress level builds, as it does around final exam time, he does not do well. As he feels this stress, Martin becomes argumentative and belligerent. He becomes suspicious of others and acts toward them as if they were his enemies. On one occasion, Martin narrowly missed having a car accident. He left his own car to chase after the other driver. The police finally were called after Martin stopped a stranger's car, broke one of the car windows, and tried to swallow the glass.

The periodic schizophrenic has more than one episode or break with reality; however, most of the time this person is able to cope fairly successfully and is able to live and work independently, with only periodic problems. These periodic flareups or "decompensations" still are unsuccessful attempts to deal with stress and change. Treatment should continue to provide structure, support, and assistance in building coping skills. The overall goal is to identify and deal with the stress that caused the present break and to restore the person's previous level of functioning.

Martin rarely comes into contact with mental health workers unless he needs hospitalization. Each time he goes into the hospital, he learns more about what he should do to avoid stress or to cope with it. His stays are shorter in duration and time is longer between admissions. Martin's career shows his increasing ability to handle the expected stresses of life.

Chronic Schizophrenia

Those with a chronic career in schizophrenia have experienced schizophrenic symptoms for longer than two years. Practically, it refers to people who have spent more of their adult lives in hospitals or treatment programs than out of them. Doug is 35 years old. He has been hospitalized over two dozen times in the last eleven years. In between hospital stays, he has attended outpatient counseling, day programs, and aftercare services. He has lived in foster care as well as on his own, in hotels and rooming houses. He also lived periodically with his aging mother. She reached the point where she felt that, physically and emotionally, she could not stand the strain of taking care of Doug.

Doug was discharged from the Army with an honorable discharge. He had won a sharpshooting medal while in the service and described the Army as "the only place where I knew what to do." About two years after leaving the military, Doug was hospitalized with schizophrenic symptoms. This was the beginning of Doug's schizophrenic career, which included multiple hospitalizations and numerous changes in his living situation. He finally was placed in a community group home, as well as in a day program. He is prescribed antipsychotic medicine, which helps him feel less anxious and permits him to act in a way that others can tolerate. Doug frequently refuses to take his medicine, claiming it is "poison." Without medication Doug hears voices that blame his failures in life on mistakes he made

during childhood. He then becomes quite agitated and pro-
ceeds to pace around the day program or his group home, with
breaks only for coffee. Doug chain-smokes, and his fingers are
stained brown from his constant contact with cigarettes. However, Doug is very different when he feels under control. Even
though his personal hygiene always seems to be a little lacking,
when he feels in control Doug is friendly and likes to help
others. Experience shows that Doug will need some type of
supervised living situation and daily supervised activity for the
rest of his life.

Symptoms in the chronic or long-term schizophrenic person
serve a slightly different purpose than they do in the acute case.
As always, symptoms arise in response to change or increased
stress. But now, the symptoms have become a way of life for the
schizophrenic. The chronic schizophrenic uses symptoms to attempt to change the environment rather than to help him or her
adapt to that environment. Such persons resist or cope with
impending stress by becoming symptomatically more disturbed.
For example, a person in a long-term treatment program will
improve gradually. During this improvement someone suggests
a move toward independent living. This might mean moving into
an apartment or getting a job. At this point, the person often will
regress and the symptoms increase in response to the stress and
upcoming change. Naturally, the job or apartment will have to
wait because of the current problem. In this manner, the chronically involved person controls the environment. This is not to
say the person enjoys or feels successful with this outcome. On
the contrary, self-esteem takes repeated beatings in the cyclical
pattern, and eventually the person takes on a role of being unable to cope with change or of being "mentally ill."

The art of working with chronic schizophrenics involves helping individuals take realistic, properly paced steps toward self-
confidence and self-reliance. In some instances, this may require
lifelong plans. Successful treatment requires great patience.

The range of emotional problems is a broad one. It is as
broad as the number of people who have problems. We all have
stress, we all have difficulty. Why do some people seem to be
made stronger by adversity, whereas others develop disabling
conditions? These issues will be examined in the next chapter.

3. *The Myths of Emotional Disturbance*
Causes

C arl discussed his emotional problems freely. He had been experiencing difficulty for quite awhile and had been diagnosed as schizophrenic for a number of years. He had an explanation for the cause of his problems. "My problems all began when I swallowed that penny."

"How's that?" I inquired.

"Well, I was fine until one day I swallowed a penny just to see what it was like. From then on I was pretty crazy and I still have trouble. Yeah, it was that penny."

Carl, like many others—including families, researchers, medical personnel, and psychologists—long have wondered what causes emotional problems. Unlike most of the others, Carl has narrowed the search to one event. He is confident about the source of his problems. However, others have developed many ideas about the causes of emotional disturbance. Many of these ideas will be explored in this chapter. Some are scientific, some are not, but all are ideas that many people believe cause emotional disturbance. First, however, emotional disturbances will be discussed in terms of what they are not.

MISTAKEN NOTIONS

Every area of human life and behavior is filled with folklore. Most of these old tales eventually are seen as untrue but are kept around for enjoyment; the tooth fairy is an example.

As people learn more about what cause and effect is, they tend to discard the old myths. However, in the area of emotional problems much misinformation is still believed.

Emotional problems are commonly called *nervous break-downs*. Although the person's functioning level may worsen, no damage actually occurs to the nerves. Emotional problems are not caused by snapping off or breaking of nerve endings. This may be a generally useful phrase but it is not descriptive of what happens to someone with emotional difficulty. There are cases where emotional stress does result in damage to body tissues, but stress does not lead to a breakdown of the central nervous system.

Emotional disturbances are sometimes confused with mental retardation. It is possible for a person to be mentally retarded and have emotional disturbances, which is known as *dual diagnosis*. A diagnosis of mental retardation refers to limited intelligence or an IQ below 70. Mental retardation also indicates an inability to take care of one's own basic needs such as dressing, eating, or hygiene. Emotionally disturbed people also may have problems with daily living, but in most cases, the emotionally disturbed person has lost these skills and abilities, whereas the mentally retarded person has never developed them. Developmental disabilities, including mental retardation, are not the same as emotional disturbances. In fact, many emotionally disturbed people are quite intelligent. However, despite their IQs, they have not been emotionally equipped to cope with the stress in their lives, and emotional problems develop.

Sexual behavior is probably the most highly charged area of human activity. People usually have strong convictions about sex, whether they are liberal or conservative. Sexuality seems to be a subject about which myths and hearsay are accepted more readily than scientific facts. Despite the work of such pioneers as Kinsey and Masters and Johnson, and more recent researchers like Shere Hite, false ideas about sexuality are common. Various sexual practices have been charged with causing madness. The sexual acts most commonly believed to lead to the development of emotional disturbance are homosexuality and masturbation. Some believe that these types of sexual conduct are symptoms of emotional problems, but there is no scientific evidence that either masturbation or homosexuality leads to psychosis or other emotional problems.

Each person must decide for himself or herself the appropriate manner or frequency of sexual activity. Since sexuality often evokes highly emotional responses from people, the possibility for emotions such as love, hate, jealousy, or guilt to be aroused as well is likely. The Victorian Era was characterized by conservative or restrictive ideas about human sexuality. Many people, then and now, develop worries and guilt over their sexual thoughts and actions, which can lead to emotional problems. Even now, society considers certain sexual practices, such as prostitution and pornography, as wrong. Strong emotions can result in deviant behavior, which may be considered as emotional disturbance, but sexual expression itself is not the cause of emotional disturbance.

Some ideas about emotional disturbance border on folklore and need to be looked at in a clearer light.

Split Personality

Over the years the emotional disturbance of schizophrenia has been confused with the separate and distinct disorder of multiple personality. In many cases, these ideas come from the media and popular literature. Books such as *The Strange Case of Dr. Jekyll and Mr. Hyde* and *Sybil* have provided many with their notion of emotional disturbance. The word *schizophrenia* literally means "split mind." The term was coined by a psychiatrist, Eugene Blueler, to indicate that normal functioning had split away from the brain. This resulted in symptoms he called *schizophrenia*. Blueler believed the most common symptoms of schizophrenia were disruptions of association and affect, autism, and ambivalence. Blueler found that the schizophrenic problem deteriorated progressively and the personality became more and more disorganized.

The multiple personality, also called a split personality, is a fairly rare disorder. People who suffer from split personality slide from one distinct personality to another distinct personality. Usually, the different personalities are not consciously aware of the process.

Both multiple personality and the schizophrenic disorders are major disturbances and both require long-term intensive therapeutic care, but they are distinct problems and should not be considered two names for the same disorder.

Increased Criminal Behavior

Emotionally disturbed individuals frequently are suspected of being more prone to commit crimes. Unfortunately, the popular conception of the emotionally disturbed is frequently based on a homicidal maniac like Norman Bates from the motion picture *Psycho*. In fact, persons experiencing emotional problems feel overwhelmed by the world around them. While some of the behaviors exhibited by emotionally disturbed people may be frightening to those around them, in reality the most frightened person is the one exhibiting the symptoms. Many of these symptoms develop from the real panic or fear that they will be swallowed up by the events that surround them, or that any relationship with others will threaten their well being. Consequently, much of this bizarre behavior is directed towards avoiding situations with which they cannot cope.

Full Moon

One of the more unusual ideas about the causes of emotional disturbance is the full moon. It is hard to say who first noticed the connection, but today, anyone who has seen a film where a man turns into a wolf during a full moon is never quite sure that the full moon does not change things in some people. More crimes tend to be committed during the full moon; emergency rooms are busier; and people in mental health settings claim to have charted increases in disordered behavior. It is clear that human functioning does follow certain cycles or patterns. There are patterns in the way people sleep, eat, work, play, wash. People do almost everything according to schedules, based on either an internal clock called *circadian rhythms* or man-made schedule keepers. It is known that the moon affects the tides, and possibly human behavior is affected by a full moon. An alternative explanation for these apparent changes is that there is more light during the full moon. With more light, people are more active and able to do more; consequently, if people are doing more, additional problem behaviors also are likely to occur.

Drugs

A drug is a substance that, once taken into the body, alters the body in some way. If the drug assists the body in fighting disease it is called a *medicine*. On the other hand, drugs are frequently taken by people for the sensations they provide. In many cases, people can relate the beginning of their emotional problems to an adverse reaction to a drug like LSD, mescaline, or cocaine—the infamous "bad trip." Certainly, prolonged use or overdose of certain drugs can result in brain damage and subsequent problems in thinking, behavior, and perception. But can small quantities of drugs cause emotional disturbance? Some say they can, claiming that one episode of drug taking resulted in all sorts of emotional problems. "I was fine until I went to this party. Somebody slipped some acid or something into my drink. I ended up in the hospital and have not been the same since." More often, however, the person struggling with emotional problems seeks to deal with these by taking drugs and blocking out reality.

The drugs have not caused the stress but pushed an already strained person over the edge. It is also possible that the same circumstances that lead to substance abuse lead also to emotional problems. The point here is that, yes, drugs can cause emotional difficulties if taken in toxic doses. It is more likely, however, that if a person taking drugs develops emotional problems, the need to take drugs is a symptom of an underlying emotional problem. The emotionally disturbed person who takes drugs may do so for a number of reasons. People may take drugs as a way of self-medicating; that is, they can handle their situation only when they are under the influence of drugs or alcohol. Alternatively, they may need the drugs less than they need the culture or the peer group that goes along with the "drug scene." The idea that drugs cause emotional disturbance subtly leads to other potentially mistaken beliefs. Namely, if some drugs were taken to cause the emotional problem, perhaps some other drugs could be taken to counteract the effects and cure the person. Certainly, in many situations medication can be useful. However, medications alone do not cure emotional disturbance. They simply alleviate the symptoms, so that the person can work on developing skills in handling relationships, stress, and change.

SCIENTIFIC THEORIES

Today, very little is believed unless scientific evidence is available to support the belief. Despite numerous studies, the experts differ on what causes emotional disturbance, but some of the areas of study will be explored here.

Genetics

It is widely accepted that the usual expectancy rate for schizophrenia in the general population is 1% to 2%. Lawrence Kallman (1953) found that if one identical twin is schizophrenic, then the chances of the other twin being schizophrenic were 86 out of 100. In fraternal twins the corresponding chances were between 3 and 17 in 100. Since identical twins have the same genes and fraternal twins do not, this study seemed to point out that genetics definitely were linked to emotional disturbance. That is, problems, or at least the susceptibility to problems, were passed on from generation to generation via their genes. While these types of studies indicate that genetics may play a part, it has not yet been established what the genetic material is or through what mechanism the material is passed from parent to child.

Biology

Ultimately, what makes a human being tick comes down to biochemistry and the interaction of chemical substances in the body. Most biological attempts at finding causes of emotional problems involve isolating a specific substance from the urine or blood of an affected person and introducing it to another person to see if symptoms begin. It is known that if a drug like

LSD is injected into the body, psychoticlike symptoms may occur. Another line of studies indicates that excess neurotransmitters in the brain result in too much brain stimulation, which can result in emotional problems. However, no one has yet definitively discovered which comes first. Do the biochemical imbalances cause the emotional problem or does emotional upset result in altered biochemistry? Regardless, the biochemical approach does show promise for the future as new discoveries are found. But current knowledge has not shown us enough to pin down any causal links.

Families

Human beings are social creatures. Much of what people do and what people are depends on their interaction with others. Everyone grows up in some type of family situation. There are theories that suggest that emotional disturbance is due in large measure to improper communication or interaction among family members. One of the most influential, developed by Theodore Lidz (1973), states that when the family fails to provide the adequate support, direction, or nurturance for a child, the child is likely to develop emotional disturbance. He felt two types of families produced disturbed offspring. The first is the skewed family, which exists to meet the needs of one of the parents, most typically the mother. The parent may not necessarily be greatly emotionally disturbed, but his or her emotional need is so great that all of the family's energy is invested in fulfilling one person's needs, and the child's needs are secondary or lost altogether.

The other type of family described by Lidz is the schismatic family, in which both parents tend to impose a distorted view of the world on the child. The parents never agree or teach the child how to act or relate to others. The child never learns how to act around others and feels overwhelmed. The child also is used to complete the parent's life or is expected to salvage the family and hold it together. Frequently, the child in this situation is never allowed to play with other children and is kept at home. Outsiders are considered bad, unhelpful, or unreliable. In both types of families, the distorted views of the parents are

presented to the offspring. The parental views on independence, intimacy, or behavior around others create in the child a
conflict so great that the child cannot function adequately.

A different pattern of parent–child interaction has been
pointed out by Gregory Bateson and his colleagues (Bateson et
al., 1956). This landmark work identified the parental form of
miscommunication called *double bind,* which is thought to prevent the child from developing the ability to make warm and
trusting relationships with others. Without this ability, interpersonal action is disrupted severely and meaningful relationships cannot be formed.

The idea of the double bind is that the parent will give the
child two separate, contradictory messages at the same time.
The child is forced to heed both messages and does not know
how to respond. For example, a mother who tells her child, "I
love you" and then recoils from the child's hug, sends the child
two messages. The overt verbal message is "I love you" and the
nonverbal message is rejection. The child is confused "Does
Mommy love me or doesn't she?" The child is not sure how to
respond, whether to respond to what the mother says or to
what she does. If this kind of miscommunication is repeated
subtly over and over again, eventually, the child will be unable
to learn how to interpret what people mean. He or she will
learn that communication does not really mean what it says.
Subsequently, the child learns that communication cannot and
should not be trusted. R. N. Suinn (1970) puts it clearly: the
double bind is "a bizarre game in which everyone agrees to
behave incomprehensibly but acts as if everything were entirely
comprehensible."

A somewhat recent theory about how families contribute to
emotional disturbance is called the *family systems approach,* in
which the person brought in with problems is only the "identified patient." Actually, the entire family is a dysfunctional system and the person with the emotional problem is only playing
one role in the system. Some therapists associated with this
approach and related techniques are Nathan Ackerman, Jay
Haley, Don Jackson, and Salvadore Minuchin. The family systems approach believes that families behave in repeated patterns, and symptoms serve as a thermostat to keep family pat-

terns from changing the established way of life. Even though the symptom obviously is painful to the person and the family, the patterns have developed over such a long period of time that the symptom has become a part of how the family interacts. All these therapists have variations on the theme, but the patient is seen to be the entire family. No longer is the "identified patient" seen as having the only problem needing change.

The Psychodynamic View

Few people would argue that the single most influential person in modern psychiatry is Sigmund Freud. Others, such as Alfred Adler, Heinz Hartman, Carl Jung, Eric Erikson, Karen Horney, Eric Fromm, and Harry Stack Sullivan, have contributed great insights and expanded Freud's work. However, Freud developed such an original and wide-sweeping theory of human behavior that even those who disagree totally with his theory use Freud's ideas as a contrast to their own.

Freud's idea is called the *psychodynamic theory,* but also has been termed the *psychoanalytic* or *intrapsychic theory.* Psychodynamic theory describes the development of the normal human personality. Emotional disturbance is seen as disruption in the normal pattern of development. Freud based his theories on two central ideas: (1) the presence and development of biological instincts or drives; and (2) the unconscious processes of the mind.

Freud believed that every child is born with drives that needed to be stimulated and fulfilled. However, the basic drives, defined as aggression and sex, cannot always be met or gratified. Deprivation of these drives or the conflict associated with drive fulfillment results in feelings of anxiety, insecurity, or guilt. In order to protect himself or herself against these negative experiences, the maturing child develops ways of coping with anxiety. This is called the *development of defense mechanisms.* Typically, a defense mechanism does not solve problems but can result in maladaptive adjustment, such as neurosis or psychosis.

The battleground for all these conflicts is the unconscious mind. Freud theorized that the unconscious is made up of three separate parts. The first part, present from birth, is the *id*. The id operates according to the "pleasure principle"; that is, it constantly seeks to satisfy the basic drives of sex and aggression. Satisfying drives reduces tension and the reduction of tension is experienced as pleasurable. Freud postulated that the id always remains in the unconscious sections of the mind and the individual remains unaware of its function.

Obviously, needs cannot always be fulfilled immediately. To deal with the real world, the second part of the personality, the *ego,* develops. The ego operates under the "reality principle." This involves thinking realistically and postponing gratification of drives. All the higher capacities like logical thinking and problem solving are under control of the ego.

Throughout the course of the child's development, he or she receives guidance and feedback on how to behave; some behavior is rewarded, some is punished. Punishment from adults around the drives of aggression and sex is experienced as highly significant. These memories are stored in the third area of the personality, the *superego.* The superego serves as a censor or conscience for the child. The superego stands in the way of the person breaking the rules and norms he or she holds internally. It is responsible for the guilt felt if various rules have been broken. The superego contains norms that sometimes can be unrealistically high or demanding. Conflict can develop if one's internal standards are unattainable. Freud felt that the personality was nearly completely developed by age 7. He felt that the child developed in a series of stages. Disruption in the normal development of stages was the cause of later emotional problems. If not treated correctly or helped to master a stage successfully, the child would become stuck, or "fixated," in that stage.

Even though the child would physically mature even into adulthood, his or her psychological-emotional development would remain in the earlier stage until it was worked through successfully. The first stage of development is the oral stage. This is derived from the fact that infants relate to the outside world via their mouths. The drives are satisfied through sucking, swallowing, and biting. Also, during the first stage, the infant is totally dependent on maternal care. If maternal care is lacking or faulty, the infant will not develop a basic sense of trust toward the world. Subsequently, the infant will not develop successful ways of relating to or trusting people in the outside world. It is suggested that infants who become stuck or fixated at this stage later develop maladaptive expressions, such as excessive smoking, excessive drinking, nail biting, and excessive dependency. As one can see, the problems are in some cases literally oral, or mouth-related, in nature. The oral stage begins at birth and lasts to around age 2. The next stage, the anal stage, begins at age 2 to 3. This is followed by the phallic stage, age 3 through 7, which is followed by the latency stage, age 7 through 12. The last stage is the genital stage, age 12 to adulthood. The theory suggests that all emotional disturbances stem from failure to successfully negotiate a particular stage.

Freud developed his own brand of therapy to assist in helping people successfully negotiate their problems. His treatment approach is called *psychoanalysis*. Although Freud used many techniques to help his patients bring out their repressed and hidden thoughts and feelings, this is very much a talking type of therapy. He used dreams, word associations, and hypnosis to help people reach back into their unconscious. Once people gained insight into the cause of their problems they could move forward into more successful thinking and behavior.

Behavioral Theories

The psychodynamic view of adaptive and maladaptive human behavior is based on internal drives and conflicts. These ideas are theories that actually cannot be witnessed, but they hold together logically and offer a believable explanation of what is happening. Behavioral theories, on the other hand, were developed from the idea that adaptive and maladaptive behavior could be explained strictly by observable and measurable events. Behaviorists believe that all behavior is learned, whether it is positive or negative. There is observable cause and effect in every case. Things such as motives, needs, and drives are not seen as valuable in explaining why people do what they do. Maladaptive behavior is learned in exactly the same ways as normal behavior. Differences lie in how often the behavior takes place, how socially acceptable and adaptive the behavior is, or the overall magnitude of the behavior. Behaviorists hold that problem behaviors can be changed by new learning or by substituting other behavior for that causing problems. Some names associated with behavioral learning theories and symptom development are B. F. Skinner, John Dollard, Neil Miller, and Albert Bandura. Others more identified with therapy by behavior modification are Joseph Wolpe and Hans J. Eysenck. There are two types of learning theorized by behaviorists. The first, termed *respondent* or *classical conditioning,* was first studied by Ivan Pavlov. In classical conditioning, an unconditioned stimulus (in Pavlov's experiments, food presented to a hungry dog) will bring an unconditioned response (salivation by the dog). A second stimulus, the conditioned stimulus (in Pavlov's case, the ringing of a bell), is paired with the unconditioned stimulus over and over again (the bell was rung as the food was presented). Eventually, the conditioned stimulus will elicit the same result as the unconditioned stimulus (the dog would salivate when the bell was rung, even if no food were presented). The response is now termed the *conditioned response.*

For example, an explanation for the emotional disturbance phobia would be explained by the behaviorists in this way: A loud noise will naturally frighten a baby. If, whenever you made that loud, frightening noise, you also showed the baby a fuzzy toy, eventually the baby would cry or be afraid and upset when only shown the fuzzy toy. The baby has learned how to be emotionally disturbed.

The second type of learning is called *instrumental* or *operant conditioning.* B. F. Skinner is associated with explaining this type of learning. In this form of learning, a person must physically do something or operate on the environment to produce some sort of effect. If the result of operating on the environment is useful, rewarding, or reinforcing to the person, the behavior is likely to be done again. Behavior can be strengthened, extinguished, changed, or modified with such reinforcement.

Problems develop when things that normally are not considered to be reinforcing or rewarding actually provide a reward.

For instance, a lonely, isolated person may wish for company or contact from others. The loneliness may become so intense and devastating that the person may begin to imagine having all sorts of friends and all sorts of power. These illusions, even though they cause great problems, give the person positive feelings, however temporary. Since the person can avoid feeling lonely by imagining friends, this sequence of events is likely to happen again.

There are many terms and extensive systems to explain behaviorism. The reader is referred to Whaley and Mallot (1968) for further details on behavioral terms and behavioral management techniques. Behavior modification has many appeals both as an explanation for emotional problems and as a basis for treatment. One appeal is its simplicity; the basic terms and ideas learned in the first day of a freshman psychology class are used and expanded upon by the most sophisticated therapist or researcher. Another advantage for behaviorism in the objective description of behavior; this emphasis on observable and measurable events is more conducive to research and therefore attractive to use.

CONCLUSIONS

This chapter briefly has described theories for causes of emotional disturbances. Many, and in some cases quite different, theories have suggested a variety of causes for emotional disturbance. What is the explanation? Perhaps this old joke can provide a clue. A psychiatrist received a telephone call. The frantic voice on the other end of the line pleaded, "Doctor, I have a big problem. Can you help me?" The doctor replied, "Well, what is your problem?" The voice, sounding more desperate, continued, "I can't explain it. If I come in and show you, will you help me?" The psychiatrist said, "Well, all right, if you can be here in 30 minutes." Ten minutes later, in the doctor's office, a man arrived with a parrot perched on his head. The doctor said, "I can see you really do have a problem." The parrot replied, "I'll say. I can't get this guy out from under my feet!"

The humor of the joke and the explanation for the various theories about emotional disturbance lie in the different perspectives and expectations of all involved. The truth is that nobody really knows for sure what causes emotional disturbance. What is known is that anything causing a person to be more distressed and to feel less able to cope is likely to cause emotional disturbance. Many studies have tried to pinpoint the causes of emotional disturbance, and each most likely describes a part of human experience, a slice of the pie called emotional disturbance. It is important, if not absolutely necessary, however, to have some notion about what causes the problems of the people treated. Practitioners treat people based on what they understand their clients' problems to be and how these problems began. Nonetheless, the practitioner's underlying theory is less important than his or her feelings. Research shows most approaches are useful as long as the person carrying it out is caring, committed, and patient. Knowledge and technique of theory is important, but a caring person who is willing to hang in there even when the going is tough is the basis of successfully treating emotionally disturbed people.

4. *The 8 A.M., Noon, and Evening Swallow*

Medications

From the beginning of time, people have searched for some potion to allay their pain and cure their ills. The fear of pain and inevitable death has motivated the creation and combination of chemicals that will make people feel more comfortable and extend their lives. As more sophisticated tools became available for understanding, analyzing, and treating the human condition, this exploration went even deeper into the intricacies of the human body. Looking toward the future, the quest for greater knowledge will be ongoing. With an ever expanding understanding of the human body, new techniques and drugs will be created to treat increasingly more complicated conditions.

OUR BODIES, OUR MINDS

Our bodies are our only birth rights. Each one is a complex mechanism of movements and responses. These mechanisms are controlled and activated by chemical and electrical impulses from both the body and the mind. As the exploration of this area progresses, perhaps, one day, it will be possible to comprehend the whole of human existence. But now, each answer leads to hundreds of new questions.

The ability to move, hear, see, feel, and think all are products of chemical reactions within the human body. How they work and interact still is a mystery, but some of the individual functions are beginning to be understood and theories of interaction are beginning to crystallize.

69

Within the physiological system, everything operates within a balance or homeostasis. One chemical excites an action and another neutralizes it, bringing the body back to homeostasis. This interrelatedness keeps the system self-regulating. These interactions among different parts of the body and mind happen chemically, by the release of hormones from glands and organs mediated or controlled by other glands or control centers in the brain. The failure of any part of this system results in disease and illness. Treatment is needed to cure the illness or at least compensate chemically for the imbalance and deficit in the body.

This disease process is particularly evident when we examine the disease of diabetes. When the pancreas cannot produce enough insulin to metabolize all the glucose or sugar taken into the body, the individual must either lower the sugar intake to what the pancreas can accommodate or take additional insulin daily to maintain homeostasis.

The intricacies of biochemical imbalances are still being explored, bringing more knowledge and answers daily about this complex field of endeavor. The neuroendocrine theory is one of many theories being considered in the cause and treatment of mental disorders. The use of psychotropic medications plays an important role in controlling the varied constellation of symptoms that individuals experience. We will discuss some of the commonest classes of medications for the treatment of emotional disturbances and briefly describe some of the symptoms treated by each.

ANTIPSYCHOTIC MEDICATIONS

Howard believed people were trying to kill him and he was suspicious of almost everyone. He would stay up all night guarding his home. Howard constantly would look out the window, attempting to see "those people" who were after him. He would lock all the doors and windows and would not leave the house for weeks at a time. Forsaking sleep and food, sometimes days at a time, he would smoke cigarettes one after another. He was afraid to leave his house, let alone try to socialize or to find work. "They are after me!" Howard insisted, but could not verbalize for what reasons. He thought that he had caused the death of some friends, who remained faceless and nameless in his past.

Howard eventually was treated with outpatient therapy and phenothiazines, which are a class of antipsychotic medications. The medications were used to decrease his visual and auditory hallucinations, paranoia, agitation, and destructive behavior.

When first given the medication, he said he was extremely tired and could not maintain his all-night vigils. This sedative quality is a common side effect of this type of medication. Although his delusions did not go away, the medication helped him control his impulses so he did not react so bizarrely to his thoughts. After several weeks, he became less tired and he began attending therapy sessions more regularly. He shaved regularly, took better care of his appearance, and in general began to feel better about himself—so much so, that eventually he began to look for work.

Without this medication, it would have been very difficult, if not impossible, to establish any type of therapeutic relationship with Howard. Medication is not an end in itself but does relieve some of the symptoms, so that the individual can begin to address the life crises and stress that make living difficult. Neuroleptic medications are divided into antipsychotic and antianxiety medications. Some medications commonly prescribed for mental health problems, as well as some possible side effects, are described briefly in Tables 4.1 and 4.2.

MEDICATION SIDE EFFECTS

All medications have side effects. Side effects are the influences that medication has on parts of the body other than the symptom being treated. Although pharmaceutical companies try to keep side effects to a minimum, the complexity of the human body is such that any new element introduced into it has an effect. Every medication targets a symptom or group of symptoms upon which to act. Sometimes, even the side effects of a medication are planned and are part of the overall treatment. If

Table 4.1
ANTIPSYCHOTIC MEDICATIONS

Trade Name	Chemical or Generic Name	Action	Side Effects
Haldol	Haloperidol	Decreases anxiety, withdrawal, hostility, hallucinations	Involuntary movements in face & hands, insomnia, headaches, confusion, blurred vision, difficulty urinating
Mellaril	Thioidazine	Decreases agitation, anxiety, depression, excitement, hyperactivity	Low blood pressure, drowsiness, restlessness, constipation, nausea, vomiting, weight gain
Thorazine	Chlorpromazine	Decreases anxiety, restlessness, apprehension, tension, hyperactivity	Low blood pressure, increased heart rate, dizziness, restlessness, uncoordinated movements, sensitivity to sunlight, dry mouth, constipation

Navane	Thiothixene	Decreases apathy, withdrawal, hallucinations, suspiciousness, anxiety, tension	Increased pulse rate, low blood pressure, rash, weakness, insomnia, dizziness, sensitivity to the sun
Prolixin Permitil	Fluphenazine	Decreases hostility, anxiety, agitation, delusions, hallucinations	Uncontrollable muscle movements, involuntary tongue movements, drowsiness, frequent urination, low blood pressure, loss of appetite
Serentil	Mesovidazine	Decreases hallucinations, tensions, anxiety, withdrawal, confusion, suspiciousness	Drowsiness, low blood pressure, rash, stiffness, restlessness, uncontrollable movements, constipation
Stelazine	Trifluoperazine	Decreases excessive anxiety, tension, agitation	Drowsiness, low blood pressure, loss of appetite, insomnia, tremors, headache, sensitivity to light

Table 4.2
ANTIANXIETY MEDICATIONS

Trade Name	Chemical or Generic Name	Action	Side Effects
Librium	Chlordiazepoxide	Relieves mild to moderate anxiety, tension	Drowsiness, low coordination ability, confusion, nausea, constipation
Valium	Diazepam	Alleviates anxiety	Drowsiness, habit forming
Seconal Tuinal	Secobarbital	Relieves mild to moderate anxiety, tension, induces sleep	Drowsiness, lethargy, habit forming, hangover
Placidyl	Ethchlorvynol	Induces sleep	Rash, nausea, hangover, habit forming, excitement, blurred vision
Equanil Miltown	Meprobamate	Relieves anxiety, tension, promotes sleep	Drowsiness, sleepiness, dizziness, slurred speech, headache, weakness, tingling in arms & legs, habit forming

an individual is having insomnia as well as an emotional disturbance, a drug may be chosen because it has a sedative side
effect as well as antipsychotic properties.

The effect of the drug sometimes filters down from the
targeted symptom and expands like a pyramid to other parts of
the body. Occasionally, the medication can interact with other
medications and create an unpredictable combination of side
effects, known as *potentiation*. This potentiation can counteract
the beneficial effect of the medication or make it dangerously
toxic.

Side effects vary in intensity and duration as a result of the
strength and type of the medication used. Most side effects are
temporary, mild, and quite common, such as sedation, constipation, or weight gain; others, such as tardive dyskinesia, are
permanent if not caught early. Tardive Dyskinesia is a "coordi-
nated, rhythmic, stereotyped, abnormal, involuntary sucking,
chewing, licking, and pursing movement of the tongue and
mouth. Grimacing, blinking and frowning are also common.
Tongue protrusion and rocking may be seen also" (Giampa,
Walker-Burt, & Finger, 1983, p. 12). Tardive dyskinesia develops only after prolonged use of certain major antipsychotic
medications and occurs in only about a third of individuals
treated with antipsychotic medications.

Efforts always are taken to stabilize an individual on minimal maintenance dosages of medication. Since the long-term
use of any medication is accompanied by risks, it is reasonable to
look for other ways to maintain an individual's stabilization.
Drug holidays, or windows, are one way of approaching this
problem. A drug holiday is a short period of time during which
an individual is taken off medication. Lowering dosages of medication is another way of decreasing side effects, but this is not to
indicate that an intermittent schedule should be used indiscrimi-
nately (Freedman, Kaplan, & Sadock, 1976). High dosages of
major antipsychotics are given only to patients during the acute
phase of their illness and are decreased to maintenance levels
after stabilization. Although antipsychotic medication does not
usually produce a permanent cure in psychotic behavior, it has
proven an effective treatment approach. With the use of medication, it has become possible to stabilize individuals within the

Table 4.3
GENERALIZED SIDE EFFECTS OF PSYCHOTROPIC DRUGS

Type of Effect	Description
Anticholinergic effects	Dryness of the mouth & throat, blurred vision, flushing, constipation, urinary retention, other autonomic side effects; effects considered mild
Extrapyramidal effects:	All these effects considered severe
Parkinsonian symptoms	Resembles Parkinson's disease: muscular rigidity, alterations of posture, tremor, masklike facial expression, shuffling gait & drooling, fatigue, lack of interest, slowness, heaviness, lack of ambition, vague bodily discomforts
Dystonias	Uncoordinated, bizarre, jerking, or spastic movements
Akathisia	Very discomforting feelings of restlessness & agitation, need to stand up, walk, tap foot, fidget
Dyskinesia	Coordinated, stereotypic, rhythmic movements. *Tardive dyskinesia* includes abnormal, involuntary sucking, chewing, licking, & pursing movements of the tongue & mouth; grimacing, blinking, frowning; tongue protrusion, rocking

community so that their adjustment to the environment can be enhanced. A medical decision to continue maintenance of an individual on medication for a long period of time is arrived at after individually assessing the person's life history and the knowledge of his or her illness. "A history of relapse after discontinuation of antipsychotic medications would be an indication of a need for a longer period of maintenance" (Freedman et al., 1976, p. 252). Table 4.3 lists some of the more common generalized side effects caused by psychotropic medications.

Cholinergic Blockers

Two other drugs, Artane and Cogentin, frequently are used with antipsychotic, antidepressant, and tricyclic medications, to block some of the adverse side effects of these medications. All antipsychotic compounds can produce extrapyramidal side effects, but cholinergic blockers suppress tremors, rigidity, and relieve other extrapyramidal symptoms. Cholinergic blockers are used only when side effects begin to emerge, and they should be used only until the individual has become stabilized on the proper dosage of medication.

For example, while on serentil, Mike had some rigidity in his arm, evident when he lowered or stretched his arm. There were short jerky movements as we tested his flexibility. He frequently would get up out of his chair and pace around the room. When he did sit down, he would shuffle his feet back and forth continuously. After taking anticholinergic medication, he was able to relax his arm more easily and smoothly. Mike then was able to feel more comfortable and sit calmly for longer periods of time.

MOOD STABILIZERS

Lithium Carbonate

Mary would go through cycles of hyperexcitement that would increase in intensity and uncontrollable impulsiveness. Her ideas would come rapidly, one after another, with only fleeting connections between them. She would go off for days, leaving her family with no explanation. When she would return, she had only vague ideas of what she had done or where she had been. As her manic behavior continued, it would move through certain patterns of excitement and remorse. During her periods of hyperactive behavior, she would not sleep for days and would become obsessed with germs. She would move all her furniture outside and wash it down with a hose in an attempt to clean her house. Then she would scrub the floors and walls with laundry soap and bleach. Obsessed with a fear of infection, she would clean herself with bleach just to kill her germs.

She was brought into a local mental health clinic by her family on the recommendation of her physician. Mary was seen by a psychiatrist, who prescribed lithium and recommended continued outpatient treatment. There were radical changes in her behavior once she was stabilized on lithium. Mary soon became more realistic about her expectations. She began considering school and preparing for a career. Although she was still nervous, she was managing at home, taking care of her children. Having been stabilized on her medication, she could live a fairly normal life-style.

Most individuals who take lithium do not complain about the side effects, since they are mild. Lithium is the treatment of choice for the manic individual and seems to prevent the reoccurrence of the extreme fluctuation in moods these individuals experience. A therapeutic dosage level can be maintained by taking the medication daily and having monthly lab tests done to determine the medication level in the blood. It is important to realize that the therapeutic level and the toxic level are very close. Therefore, the individual must be monitored frequently in a controlled setting while being stabilized on the medication. After the individual is stabilized he or she can be maintained in an outpatient setting very successfully.

ANTIDEPRESSANTS

MAO Inhibitors

Ruth, a 62-year-old woman with a long history of hospitalizations, would pace the floor all night, wringing her hands and sobbing. She would not dress or bathe herself regularly. She would refuse to eat or leave her house for months at a time. Her voice was pressured and quivering as she spoke. She would resist any attempts by others to help her. Ruth knew she was guilty of something for which she never could be forgiven. She was obviously suffering, hopelessly enveloped in her own private misery.

Ruth had an endogenous or internally induced depression, with no apparent external cause. It was as though she was overwhelmed by her physical sensation of misery. She was seen by a psychiatrist and was treated with a class of antidepressant medications called *monoamine oxidase (MAO) inhibitors*. Although other antidepressive medications were tried, none seemed to be as effective as this type for her condition. Her personal hygiene improved; she began to dress up, go out for dinner, and to the senior citizens center to play cards every Tuesday night. Eventually, she even volunteered at a local church to help set up for its special events. MAO inhibitors had provided her with enough relief from her misery to have her feel better about herself and occasionally laugh and smile.

A warning should be indicated here. Large amounts of this type of medication, taken at one time, can be extremely dangerous and toxic. This is of particular importance with potentially suicidal individuals. Thus, evaluating the suicide potential of the depressed person should be ongoing.

Taking this MAO medication also requires dietary restrictions. People are required to avoid foods containing the chemical tyramine. This chemical is frequently found in common foods like aged cheese, chocolate, sour cream, beer, red wine, and anything else that requires a fermentation process. A careful list of "forbidden" foods should be prescribed by the physician or dietitian. An individual on MAO inhibitors who consumes foods containing tyramine runs the risk of side effects that range from headaches to extreme hypertensive (high blood pressure) episodes, which can be fatal. "The hypertensive crisis usually begins with a severe headache that starts suddenly, and is usually located at the back of the head. Vomiting, fever, chest pains, muscle twitching, and restlessness also are present in this syndrome. This attack usually disappears in a few hours without complications, but it may cause intracranial bleeding, which could be fatal" (Barchas, 1977, p. 198).

Tricyclic Antidepressants

Mac had to retire when he was disabled because of back problems. He was depressed because he had lost all his retirement money and was having some major problems paying his bills. Mac would not get out of bed for weeks at a time. He felt totally helpless and out of control of his life. Mac knew what he needed to do but could not find the energy to fight with life anymore. He felt angry about his situation yet did not show signs of contemplating suicide. Mac has a reactive depression, in response to external influences, physical problems coupled with financial difficulties.

He was treated with a tricyclic antidepressant medication to allay some of his suffering. As with most people, Mac gradually began to respond to the medication and within two weeks was feeling less depressed. Mac was able to work around the house occasionally and find some odd jobs as a welder to make some additional money. He was able to get out of the house and go fishing without being overwhelmed by his feelings of depression and hopelessness. In the therapeutic setting, he began to address some of his adjustment and financial concerns and was able to bring these problems under control. He now held more hope for the future.

Mac was told not to drink alcohol while on the medication. Alcohol has the effect of potentiating the harmful side effects of this particular drug. Potentiation of drugs with other drugs increases their potency and effect on the body. This is particularly true with the combination of tranquilizers, antidepressants, and alcohol. But this also is true with most drugs; individuals under treatment should be advised not to consume any alcohol while taking medication. Like any other medication, tricyclics have a number of side effects. In this case, Mac complained of a dry mouth. Other side effects include palpitations, fainting, dizziness, vomiting, constipation, and edema (swelling).

Tricyclic antidepressants are considered much safer than MAO inhibitors and usually they are just as effective in the treatment of depression. Three of the most commonly prescribed tricyclic antidepressants are tofranil, norpramin, and sinequan. Table 4.4 describes some of the major antidepressants.

STIMULANTS: RITALIN

Steven, a hyperactive child, was always on the move. His teacher considered him a disciplinary problem, but did not know how to handle him. He could not sit still and was always

81

Table 4.4
TRICYCLIC ANTIDEPRESSANTS

Trade Name	Chemical or Generic Name	Action	Side Effects
Tofranil	Imipramine	Reduces depression	Increased pulse rate, lowered or elevated blood pressure, confusion, restlessness, insomnia, tremors, tingling in arms or legs, constipation, sensitivity to sunlight, excess perspiration, loss of appetite
Norpramin Pertofrane	Desipramine	Reduces depression	Increased pulse rate, numbness in arms or legs, tremors, urinary retention, blurred vision, sensitivity to sunlight, dizziness, perspiration, lack of coordination
Sinequan	Doxepin	Reduces depression, anxiety, fear, insomnia	Drowsiness, constipation, dizziness, rash, increased perspiration, edema, numbness in arms or legs, weight gain
Elavil	Amitriptyline	Reduces depression, anxiety	Drowsiness, blurred vision, dryness of mouth, constipation, impaired urination, rash

out of his chair. His mother reported that he was always on the go, all over the neighborhood. It was as though he had a motor running. Even a television program could not hold his attention and keep him from moving around. She reported that sometimes he would be up all night unable to unwind and settle down. After Steven was assessed as hyperactive, he was given a drug called Ritalin. Ritalin is a stimulant that has been successful in the treatment of hyperactive children.

It seems odd that stimulants, such as Ritalin, would be used to control hyperactivity, but nevertheless, this treatment has met with success. A number of theories have been proposed that attempt to explain this unexpected phenomenon.

The first theory states that the real problem with the hyperactive child is that he or she is underaroused and Ritalin provides the necessary stimulation to increase the individual's alertness to the environment. The second theory proposes that because of glandular malfunctions within the physical system, the medication triggers the natural antagonist to the stimulation. This brings the metabolism back to homeostasis or the normal condition. The third theory states that adding a stimulant to the individual's already stimulated system floods the brain with so much stimulation that it actually blocks any further arousal in the child. As can be seen, the actual knowledge of why a medication works is still hampered by the limited understanding of both the human body and the human condition.

MEDICATION SAFETY

Individuals taking medications such as these must be supervised and monitored. Therefore, those caring for them should be aware that any medication can be dangerous if it is used improperly. Certain precautions should be followed in order to assure the safe administration of medications. Locking all medications and maintaining a current inventory is not only a safe practice, it also is a necessary one. In cases of emergency, this may help you determine what and how much of a medication was taken.

The person administering medication should always check the medication log for the person's name, the medication being given, dosage, and the prescribed time to be administered. Read the medication label once when removing the medication from the cabinet. Read it again when administering the proper dosage. Then read it once more when putting the medication away. Safety cannot be overemphasized. Never leave medications unattended for any period of time. Always lock the cabinet after dispensing the medication. You are protecting the entire household or program from the dangers of a drug overdose.

Do not force individuals to take medication, but note any refusal to take medication and refer this information to the physician. The decision to give the medication against a person's will requires a court order that specifies that the individual would be harmful to himself or herself or to others without the medication (Giampa et al., 1983).

No matter how much care is taken, mistakes can occur. Due to the potential seriousness of medication errors, prompt action must be taken. Medication can be fatal if it is not taken properly, so emergency steps to cope with a medication error clearly must be in place. Do not ignore the situation; call immediately for help. Notify the physician and the hospital. Inform them what has happened and have your facts right regarding what medication was taken, dosage, to whom, and whether that individual is on any other type of medications. The physician or nurse will take it from there. Answer all their questions. Confidentiality does not apply in a life-threatening situation. Listen carefully to their instructions and write them down. You probably will be asked to monitor and observe the individual until help arrives or to provide emergency first aid through the critical period of risk.

Ideally, no emergency or error will ever happen, but it is always good to be prepared for such a circumstance. Every supervisor should prepare procedures to follow in such an event. A few recommendations are

1. Have the hospital, police, and ambulance numbers close to the phone.
2. Have the number of the local Poison Control Center. It is

available from a local hospital or the *Physicians' Desk Reference.*

3. Know the number of the individual's personal physician.
4. Have people trained in CPR and advanced first aid. These skills not only are important professionally but are invaluable in personal life as well.

Preparing for an emergency and being careful are the best ways of preventing a mistake from turning into a tragedy.

PHYSICIANS' DESK REFERENCE

The *Physicians' Desk Reference* (PDR) is a helpful reference book to have available wherever medications are administered. It provides a comprehensive listing and description of each prescribed medication currently on the market. This resource book is published annually with periodic supplemental updates.

The PDR reference guide is very easy to use. The simplest approach is to page through the rose colored section, which lists the product names in alphabetical order. After you have located the medication's name, there will be two numbers following this listing. The first number refers to the photographic section of the book for quick identification. The next number refers to the description of the medication.

Within the description portion of this guide, there are a number of important areas to become familiar with:

1. The medication name appears in bold print.
2. Next is listed the usual method of dispensation of the medication.
3. The next section gives a brief description of why the medication is used.
4. The next section describes contraindications of why the medication would not be prescribed. There also are warnings about the medication here.
5. The following sections are useful lists of adverse reactions followed by overdose manifestations. These sections are important if you are ever asked to observe and monitor an

individual taking these medications. They indicate the possible side effects of the medication, starting with the most
common and continuing to the least common side effect.
6. The final section refers to the usual dosages given.

This pattern is followed fairly consistently throughout the
PDR. It would be wise to become familiar with the entire
description of the medication in question, as there is quite a bit
of helpful information within this resource book.

Usually, after the photographic identification section is a
directory of Poison Control Centers throughout the United
States. Find the closest one and write the number down near the
phone. This may prove to be invaluable during an emergency.

In conclusion, medication is important for the stabilization
of the emotionally disturbed individual. Furthermore, it makes
community placement possible and practical for the individual
and our society. Although medication must be coupled with
therapy in the treatment of the whole individual, it does serve
as a starting point for normalization.

As with anything, certain risks must be considered when an
individual is on medication. Staff members must be constantly
vigilant of these risks, from side effects to dependence. Their
observations can be helpful to the treating physician. Medication is a complex treatment modality and professionals, including physicians and nurses, have spent years studying their effects and uses. It is best to refer all questions regarding the use
of medications to the treating physicians. It is helpful if paraprofessionals observe behavior, possible side effects and other
changes the individual may exhibit and relay this information
to the physician for possible clinical consideration.

5. *What Not to Do and Why*
Ethics

*P*eople who choose to work in the field of mental health need to respect the dignity and worth of the individuals they help and to strive for the preservation and protection of fundamental human rights. Those who work in this field must realize that they bear a heavy social responsibility because their actions may alter the lives of others. Every effort must be made to protect the welfare of those who seek such services.

Whether the work is done in group homes, hospitals, day treatment centers, or other community agencies committed to assisting those in need, it is of utmost importance that the jobs be performed with the highest ethical standards and principles. Ethics concerns the "rightness" or "wrongness" of human actions and issues of good and bad (Van Hoose & Kottler, 1982). Ethics is a standard of conduct in relation to others. This chapter outlines forms of behavior that are improper and explains why such behavior should not be engaged in. Engaging in sexual activity, supplying nonprescribed drugs, and abusing an individual's human rights will be the central focus of this chapter. Individuals in treatment are very vulnerable, and because of this, those who treat them must abide by the highest ethical standards.

SEX

Rape is an act of sexual intercourse by means of force, threat, or deception. It is illegal. Unfortunately, we hear all too often of disturbed individuals being sexually abused by those they have come to trust. If a worker in the mental health field engages in sexual activity with an individual under his or her care, this is an act of rape. It is not a minor crime but a very serious and profound one. The punishment for rape, of course, is imprisonment.

Emotionally disturbed individuals are very needy people. They often are very frightened and confused. Many are unloved. All have a desperate need to make sense of their world. As often happens when working with the emotionally disturbed, caretakers begin to develop a relatively close relationship with these individuals. Over time, trust may begin to develop, accompanied by the natural emotions of warmth, closeness, and caring.

The trust that develops is a sign of a job well done. It is very possible that these individuals have trusted no one in a very long time. These confused and frightened people feel grateful that somebody finally understands and cares about them; they feel secure. They may begin to develop feelings of love, trust, and caring. They even may begin to get better.

Unfortunately, there are some people in all professions who behave unethically. These people, whether operating out of ignorance of the ethical consequences of their acts or out of conscious manipulation to attain personal goals, are dangerous to the welfare of those who seek their services and threaten the effectiveness of their institutions, the integrity and reputation of their colleagues, and the stability of their professions. Take for example the hospital aide who bragged about how many women patients he had been involved with sexually. He thought of himself as quite a man because of his ability to seduce so many women. As we can see, this individual operated out of ignorance and manipulation. He manipulated the women patients for his own personal goals, and he operated out of ignorance because he bragged to other hospital personnel about his "manly feats." This individual did not consider what consequences his sexual behavior had on the emotional stability of the patients. The patients had put their trust in him because they believed he was there to help them. Unfortunately, he exploited his relationship with these patients. It is very possible that because of this person's behavior some of these individuals will have a very difficult time trusting anyone again.

Becoming personally involved is an ethical conflict frequently encountered by those who work in the caring professions. Emotionally disturbed individuals sometimes attempt sexual seductions. Transference and countertransference dynamics (discussed in Chapter 6) and outside social encounters with clients all are experiences that must be faced on a regular basis. Unfortunately, dealing with the impulses and emotions aroused by a sexually or personally attractive individual is a skill that is difficult to learn. Hard work is involved in restraining the honest and spontaneous desire to love another person who is attractive.

Judy worked in a day treatment center. She was single, shy, and had difficulty in her own personal relationships with men. Mike, who had recently been released from the hospital, began attending the center. Mike was very handsome, quite bright, had a good sense of humor, and also was somewhat shy. Judy was immediately attracted to Mike and began seeing him after she got off work. Within a month Judy was pregnant. She did not know what to do or to whom to turn. She told Mike that she was pregnant. One week later Mike had a psychotic episode and needed to be rehospitalized. It is very possible that Mike's psychotic episode was related to the pressure of finding out that he was going to become a father. Judy should never have become sexually involved with Mike.

Sam worked in a group home and was extremely attracted to Liz, who was a resident at the home. Liz was a very attractive young woman, but she also had some serious emotional difficulties. Sam was transferred to another group home in the area and began to date Liz. This is an unethical situation, because Sam once worked at the group home where Liz lived. He had the ability to look at her private records, know her history, discuss her problems at staff meetings, and as a staff member had "authority" over her. Liz, on the other hand, did not have Sam's case history, did not discuss Sam's personal problems at staff meetings, and was dependent on his authority. Because Sam was a kind and caring person who tried to understand and help Liz, she naturally began to care for him. It is hard work to restrain the natural desire to love another person who is attractive and who returns the affection, but such a relationship is not permissible. As can be seen, such a relationship is based on deception. Liz did not really know Sam; she knew only his image and the image of Sam she created in her own mind. It was Sam's job to be patient, caring, understanding, kind, and helpful. Sam was also in a position of authority, which created dependency in Liz. At first, Sam was sexually attracted to Liz, but later, he was emotionally attracted to her dependency on him. Both Sam and Liz were attracted to aspects in each other that were created by the environment in which they were situated. The relationship was based on deception. Sam did not intentionally try to deceive Liz, although he did not think through the relationship. He was ignorant of the fact that his very position as a worker in a group home placed him in an authoritative position over the residents in the home. Unfortunately, there are some individuals who intentionally manipulate this situation to meet their own sexual needs. In these situations, the worker is considered to have raped the resident and to have committed a very serious crime. If you know or work with anyone who engages in this unethical behavior it is your ethical duty to report this behavior to your supervisor.

DRUGS

In this section a drug is defined as any chemical substance used for "recreational" purposes. This includes alcohol, marijuana, and many other chemical substances. As self-evident as it might seem, practitioners should not use drugs with those who have come seeking help. Unfortunately, some individuals respond to this rule in an unethical manner. Take for example the group home worker who went out drinking with her residents. It was a hot summer day and the residents were just getting back from a shopping trip. One of the residents suggested that they go to the local bar for a couple of beers. At first the worker said no, but finally after all of the residents pressured her, she gave in, and they all went to the bar. The day went very well and everyone had a good time. What was unethical about this?

A number of things. First, all of the residents were on some form of medication. Through the years, their doctors had told them not to mix alcohol with medicine. This worker was giving the residents a completely contradictory message. Through her actions she was saying it was alright to drink even while taking medication. The residents were given a double message: they were caught between two authorities giving two totally different messages. The residents will stay confused on this point. Second, the worker did not realize that two of the residents were alcoholics. By her actions she was encouraging these individuals to drink alcohol. Finally, she is a role model; that is, an individual whose behavior should be respected and imitated. Under the circumstances drinking alcohol was not a behavior that should be respected and imitated by these individuals.

Sometimes our insecurities will force people into behaving unethically. All people want to be liked, and this is especially true for those who work in the mental health field. It is much easier for a practitioner to work with an emotionally disturbed individual who likes him or her than with one who does not. For example, Greg was a van driver for a day treatment center. He was taking six people on a field trip into the city. About halfway there Greg smelled marijuana coming from the back of the van. Greg asked who was smoking marijuana. Apparently everyone in the van was smoking and they asked Greg if they could finish the "joint." Greg said no at first, but he was then immediately accused of not being "hip," "cool," a "good guy." Greg was in a dilemma. He wanted to be liked by these individuals, because he knew that if they disliked him his job would be much harder. He let the individuals finish smoking.

Greg's behavior was unethical. First, smoking marijuana currently is against the law. Second, even though Greg did not smoke, he "let" those who were in his care smoke, thus indicating to them that he needed their approval. Finally, by stepping out of his role as caregiver, Greg became an unwilling co-conspirator. He and the others were now in alliance against the other authority figures at the center. Greg now found that he had a new role at the center; he was neither a "staff member" nor a "patient." Greg was confused and so were the other individuals at the program. Greg's need for approval ended up in a problem situation.

Workers in the field of mental health should not sell, buy, encourage, or participate in the usage of drugs with those individuals who seek assistance. Practitioners are free to act in any manner they choose outside of work, that is their time. However, at work, they need to be especially aware of acting in a responsible and ethical manner. Those who cannot abide by such ethical principles are in the wrong line of work. Mental health workers bear a heavy social responsibility because their actions can alter the lives of others.

HUMAN RIGHTS

Unethical people may be described as those who lack sufficient integrity, moral commitment, and sound judgment to maintain standards of right and wrong in their particular line of work. They may be unaware of or unconcerned about the ethical standards of their professions and ignorant of the possible negative effects of their behavior. In acting out of ignorance, inadequate training, self-interest, or faulty judgment, an individual may be following unethical practices (Schwebel, 1955).

Individuals who engage in unethical practices without even being aware of the damage they may inflict are considered incompetent. *Incompetence* can be defined as lacking the skill, ability, or qualifications to responsibly and effectively carry out a task. Failure to recognize one's fallibilities and limitations also are elements of incompetence. Because of the nature of the work, practitioners need to be especially sensitive to their own and others' behavior. They work with human beings, not with machines, and because of this, they need to respect human rights.

The remainder of this chapter will focus on seven aspects of human rights requiring special sensitivity: confidentiality, physical intervention, putting the focus on oneself, imposing personal values on the individual, medication, commitment, and behavior therapy.

Confidentiality

Confidentiality means keeping private or secret any information obtained from or about an individual who has come to us seeking assistance. This includes not disclosing or divulging any information at all about clients without their expressed permission in writing—not even the individual's name, address, phone number, or personal characteristics. Practitioners do not discuss with their friends certain aspects of their work: the interesting individual who recently has been admitted to the program, the strange behavior witnessed, or the funny things the individual said or did that day. Individuals who suffer from emotional disturbance have the right to privacy. It is unethical to discuss an individual's problems outside of the treatment setting.

Intentional or unintentional breaches of confidentiality can occur for a number of reasons. Intentional breaches of confidentiality are necessary to protect the individual's welfare or to protect an endangered party who may be threatened by a potentially dangerous individual. For example, a practitioner who discovers that an individual has or will commit a violent crime must inform others. This also would be true if the individual is sexually, physically, or emotionally abusing children or threatening suicide.

Unintentional breaches of confidentiality can occur when one simply makes a mistake and inadvertently lets something slip out. For example, after work, several nurses from the psychiatric unit of the hospital went out to the local tavern to relax after a hard day at work. After a while, they began talking about a number of patients at the hospital. To their surprise, at the very next table sat the parents of one of the individuals they were talking about. This, of course, was a very embarrassing situation for all those involved.

All people need to relax after a hard day at work, but the need to discuss happenings at work should take a back seat to the individual's right to confidentiality. If asked if a certain individual is attending a program, professional caretakers simply say that they cannot give out that information. The right to privacy is a fundamental human right, which should be respected and never be abused. Some of the ways in which the rights of confidentiality can be violated include the following:

1. Talking about a disturbed individual with family and friends.
2. Identifying a person as belonging to a program when meeting outside of work.
3. Referring to a second individual in the program by full name, when charting on an individual or discussing an individual with his family, teachers, or other nonstaff persons.
4. Taking photographs without permission or listening-in on phone conversations.
5. Discussing information in the individual's record with people who are not authorized to obtain this information.
6. Releasing information without proper authorization or Release of Information form.

Physical Intervention

Physical intervention or physical management is the use of physical force by staff members against clients. Staff use approved techniques in order to physically protect the client from substantially harming him or herself or others. There are times when it is necessary to use physical intervention; however, such practices should be used only in extreme emergencies. Physical intervention should be used in conjunction with other, nonphysical intervention and only as a last resort. The use of physical management techniques is appropriate only to prevent injury to the individual or other persons or to prevent substantial damage to property. The *least restrictive* technique is to be used, with the safety of the client being a primary concern. To restrain someone physically, without sufficient reason, is a breach of his or her right as a human being.

John works at a psychiatric hospital. He bragged about and found it humorous every time he had to tie someone up in leather restraints. In fact, he found this so entertaining that occasionally he would purposely upset an individual so that he could use physical intervention. Obviously, John had some very severe emotional problems and his behavior was extremely unethical.

Putting the Focus on Oneself

There are times when it is beneficial to discuss one's own personal difficulties and use examples from one's own life to highlight a principle for another individual's benefit. Self-disclosure can be a very effective way to promote the therapeutic relationship, to illustrate a point, to model effective problem solving, and to show that all human beings have problems. Use caution, however; taking the focus off the individual and putting it on oneself exclusively means abusing the individual and behaving unethically. The individuals did not come to the program to listen to the practitioner's problems; they came to get assistance with their own. Following this same line of thought, practitioners do not put their own interests over the interests of the individual. If, for example, a staff member wants to attend a certain field trip for personal reasons and the majority of individuals in the program do not want to attend this field trip, it would be highly unethical to go on this field trip. During working hours, the needs of the individuals seeking assistance come before the practitioners' own personal needs.

Joan worked in an aftercare program and was involved in many group therapy sessions. Over a period of time, she found out that Sally, one of the individuals in the group, was trying to sell some oceanfront property. Sally was having some difficulty selling this property. Joan was very interested in oceanfront property and began to discuss the prospect of buying this property from Sally at a reduced rate. Fortunately, Joan's supervisor found out about this and informed Joan that such a transaction would not be very ethical. Emotionally disturbed individuals generally are vulnerable to exploitation. In this case, Sally needed to show Joan that she cared for her and the reduced rate was her way of making this point. It would have been unethical for Joan to accept such a valuable gift because she would be taking advantage of Sally's natural positive regard for Joan as a staff member. In fact, as a general practice, it is unwise to accept any gifts that are offered by those seeking assistance. There have been cases where gifts have been accepted that were worth much more than their face value. In these cases, embarrassing situations followed. In many cases, a gift means much more than just a gift. A gift could mean now you owe me something; or let's not keep a working relationship but develop a friendship and more; or because I gave you this you should like me and treat me differently from the others; or I deserve more of your time; you can do favors for me; more gifts will come if you treat me differently; or a host of other unsaid, hidden meanings. As can be seen, sometimes a gift may mean more than just thanks.

Of course, there are times when an individual really needs to show appreciation for the services received. In these cases, the gift should be accepted on the part of the entire center. It should be made clear that the gift will be shared and enjoyed equally by everyone at the facility. In refusing to accept a gift from an individual, practitioners always acknowledge that they are honored and flattered by the show of affection but are honored even more by the client's improved condition, and a gift of appreciation is not necessary.

Imposing Personal Values on the Individual

Imposing one's own values and beliefs on an individual is another unethical behavior commonly engaged in but rarely questioned. Do workers in the field of mental health have the right to impose their own values on the individuals who have come seeking assistance? If in my treatment plan I suggest that John Smith should "develop better interpersonal skills and socialize with more people," who am I to say this is what John Smith needs? Maybe it is what I need. Maybe John Smith enjoys his privacy and prefers only a few close friends. Everyone has an individual set of personal values, and it may be unethical to instruct others on how they should live their lives.

Medication

Medication has proven to be extremely effective in helping emotionally disturbed individuals cope with life. However, as with any treatment, it is essentially up to the individual whether he or she would like to accept this form of treatment. All medication has side effects. Some side effects can be quite serious. In most cases, it is unethical to force an individual to take medication. In some cases, the workers or caretakers generally are more relieved when an extremely disruptive individual begins taking medication. It is unethical to force an individual to take medication if it only means that the work of others will become less disrupted. Many states are now beginning to create laws where medication can be given against a person's will only if that person is in immediate danger of hurting himself, herself, or others, or is damaging property.

Commitment

Commitment is the involuntary placement of an individual into a mental hospital. It is a legal procedure in which a petition is filed with the probate court, and the individual is judged to be incompetent prior to commitment to a mental hospital. Each state has its own laws and rules on the procedure. When individuals are committed to a hospital, many of their rights are taken away. Once judged incompetent, the police may be called to take the individual to the hospital, forcibly if necessary. Because of this, commitment is a very serious and ethically determined procedure. Obviously, petitions are not filed and people are not forced into mental hospitals except as a last resort; this would be a highly unethical thing to do. First all other available alternatives must be explored.

Behavioral Therapy

Behavioral therapy is a form of treatment where rewards and punishments are utilized to shape an individual's behavior. In institutional settings and in individual clinical interventions, behavioral procedures frequently have proved more successful than other techniques. However, behavior therapy can be abused and turned into a violation of ethical and legal principles. When aversive control techniques, such as painful stimulation, are used to shape an individual's behavior or if that individual is deprived of some basic privilege, such techniques have been looked upon as unethical and even illegal. Punishment by aversive stimuli and deprivation of basic privileges have been judged in some cases as improper and questionable on constitutional grounds (Van Hoose and Kottler, 1982).

Another frequent criticism is that reinforcement techniques amount to bribery. That is, some reinforcement techniques are unethical and produce only temporary behavioral changes, since the individual may work mainly for the reward. In addition, "shaping" an individual's behavior means telling the individual how to live his or her life and what is best for him or her. In using behavioral techniques several questions should be asked: Are we sure we know what is right or wrong? What is best for this individual? How should this individual live his or her life? Many professional associations are moving to prevent abuses by setting up behavior modification committees to deal with pertinent questions in a range of settings. Experts decide if such treatment is called for and if alternative, less restrictive plans can be attempted.

Anyone who works in the field of mental health bears a heavy social responsibility. Those who choose to work in this field are committed to assist others in need and, therefore, must enter their jobs with the highest ethical standards and principles. They work with very vulnerable individuals, and because of this vulnerability, emotionally disturbed individuals are sometimes exploited. This chapter briefly outlined some of the more outstanding practices that are considered unethical. Engaging in sexual activity with those who seek assistance is an extremely serious crime and should be dealt with in the strictest manner. Selling, buying, encouraging, or participating in the use of drugs with emotionally disturbed individuals is a highly unethical practice. Workers in the field of mental health support, practice, and encourage all aspects of human rights.

Nobody is perfect and everyone, at one time or another, may have engaged in some form of unethical practice. People must learn from their mistakes and strive for continued growth and improvement. The field of mental health is a very interesting one, but at the same time it can be very demanding and draining. Because of this, only very unique and special people are attracted to this field. Generally, such people are warm, caring, giving, and honest individuals concerned with the human condition, with life, and with the continued improvement of humanity. Because of these characteristics, they are above average. In actuality it is rare when an extremely unethical situation occurs in this field. But, everyone in it must continue to strive for higher ethical standards and show the rest of society that the field is an important one, on the forefront of progressive change.

TWO

Practice, or How It Is Done

6. *The COUNT System*

Tom paced the floor, walking back and forth all day long, repeating the word *what*. "What . . . What . . . What . . . What . . . What . . . ," nonstop, all day long, repetitiously. Of course, asking Tom "what" he was doing would only increase his repetitions. You see, Tom had found the secret of the universe in the word *what*. Tom believed he was Jesus Christ and that he was spreading the gospel truth through his words.

Tom, like many other people who are given the label *schizophrenic,* is extremely terrified of others. In his seemingly bizarre behavior, Tom was doing an incredibly competent job of isolating himself from people. Whenever Tom acted in such a bizarre manner, no one wanted to be around him. It must be understood that Tom did not choose to act this way in a conscious manner, but unconsciously and without intentionally doing so, he had found a strategy for isolating himself from others. Tom, in a strange and ironic way, had indeed found the secret of his universe. If put under stress, Tom automatically began acting in this bizarre manner, isolating himself from people, and thus securing the peace he needed. Tom was telling others through his actions that he needed an environment that was consistently safe, secure, and trustworthy.

Mary never moved. She just sat there. If she did talk at all, it usually was only one or two words, and this was done with extreme difficulty. You see, Mary was the type of person you could easily forget about. She just blended into the walls. Mary never caused any trouble; however, some people were concerned by her unresponsiveness. By this time, people were convinced that Mary would never get any better. She, too, was labeled *schizophrenic*. Observing Mary over time taught us, however, that even if the situation appears hopeless, one should never lose one's sense of optimism. By being natural and honest, a practitioner often can tempt an individual away from their withdrawn disillusionment and begin the development of an open and trusting relationship.

Jim sat in the corner of the room with his head down, sleeping. This was what Jim did most of the day. An unusually large man, he was approximately 5'10" tall and weighed almost 300 pounds. Jim spoke rarely and then only in short sentences. His hygiene was extremely poor, hair oily and clothing soiled; he often drooled from the corner of his mouth. Through the years, Jim had received the standard treatment procedures including electroshock therapy and intravenous administration of psychotropic medication. Apparently, nobody ever had bothered to establish an interpersonal relationship with Jim. A consistently unbiased, natural, and optimistic interpersonal approach would have been far better than any treatment Jim ever received.

These examples of individuals suffering from extreme disturbances of emotion are presented to illustrate how difficult it may seem to reach individuals on a therapeutic level. In all people's lives, there will be times of depression, anxiety, and uncertainty; however, these emotions differ significantly from those experienced by Tom, Mary, and Jim. When most people feel emotionally upset, they can turn to friends, relatives, or other significant people in their lives. The period of emotional upheaval generally is short-lived, and they usually continue with the routine of their daily lives.

Tom, Mary, Jim, and others like them cannot turn to anyone. Generally, these individuals have lived lives full of ambiguity, inconsistency, and uncertainty; they have learned not to trust the world around them. The symptoms, the behavior that can be observed, often is very disturbing to those around them. However, it must be remembered that the individual who suffers from extreme disturbances of emotion has an incredibly difficult time trusting others and is quite frightened of people.

In Chapter 3, in the section on the causes of schizophrenia, it was pointed out that some theories suggest that the individual who becomes schizophrenic experiences a life in which it virtually is impossible to develop a sense of basic trust. The symptoms of the schizophrenic individual are seen as a basic defensive maneuver for self-preservation. Behavior such as extreme withdrawal, bizarre acting-out behavior, and seemingly incomprehensible verbalizations all are excellent maneuvers to keep people away. The individual who suffers such extreme disturbances of emotion has been hurt and does not want to be hurt again.

When people are upset, they may want to hide, or scream obscenities, or behave in other ways that they later regret. During such momentary periods of upset, individuals generally do not like themselves very much and consider others even worse. Now, the emotional disturbance within a psychotic individual is increased a hundredfold; in addition, this is no momentary reaction to problems but a lifetime reaction. That is, a psychotic individual can be in a state of extreme disturbance 24 hours a day, 7 days a week, 365 days a year.

So, how can someone reach such a disturbed person? At first it may seem impossible; there may seem to be countless things to do. In fact, researchers have found that there are really only five. The COUNT system was designed not so much for the individuals going through extreme emotional disturbances but for understanding the emotional aspects within all people. The five guidelines to follow in order to deal most effectively with those suffering emotional disturbances are these:

1. Be extremely *consistent* with the individuals with whom you work.
2. Have an *optimistic* outlook on life and on the future.
3. Be *unbiased* with whomever you are working.
4. Be *natural,* be yourself.
5. Ultimately, develop a basic sense of *trust* within the individual with whom you are working.

COUNT stands for consistency, optimism, unbiased attitude, naturalness, and trustworthiness.

This chapter is designed to help practitioners deal most effectively with emotionally disturbed individuals. The COUNT system is a total system that forces one to look at one's own emotions and personality. It is our conviction that those who cannot live up to the ideals outlined in this chapter, in fact, may be in the wrong line of work. Working with emotionally handicapped individuals can be a very rewarding experience, rarely boring and always fascinating; however, it takes very special people. The emotionally disturbed individual is one of the most vulnerable members of society today. It takes a person who is sensitive, emotionally mature, and maintains a basic self-respect and love of others to have the caring and patience to relate to such disturbed and vulnerable individuals.

CONSISTENCY

Each one of the COUNT factors for working with emotionally disturbed individuals is important; however, consistency seems to be of primary importance. As described in Chapter 3, the environment in which the schizophrenic person is raised is often filled with extreme inconsistencies in communication. Caught in a "double-bind" situation (Bateson et al., 1956), the individual always feels trapped into doing the wrong thing, no matter what he or she does. Theoretically, the individual who will later be labeled *schizophrenic* grows up in a family in which the parents always say one thing on the overt, verbal level, yet imply a contradictory meaning on another level. Any message obeyed at one level is disobeyed at the other.

Chapter 3 also cited the theory suggesting that schizophrenia occurs when the egocentric needs of either one or both of the parents interferes with the child's emotional development (Lidz, 1973). Once again, throughout his or her development, the child is given inconsistent double messages that often are extremely confusing and upsetting. It was shown that the child who is to develop an emotional disturbance enters adolescence unable to cope with the developmental tasks of achieving independence from these parents. In all of these theories, it is suggested that the seeds of schizophrenia are spread by a life-time of inconsistent messages given to the developing child.

Now, it is no remarkable insight that an individual who is exhibiting severely disturbed symptoms would be even more disturbed by inconsistent messages. The best way to avoid the trap of giving inconsistent messages is for one to always follow through with whatever has been said. For example, if an area is designated as nonsmoking, then this always is a nonsmoking area. If sometimes an individual is allowed to smoke there and sometimes not, the rules are inconsistent; the disturbed person once again is getting double messages and remains confused. What is said or done is important; however, the words and actions need to be consistent with each other. If a certain rule has been broken, be consistent in the consequences specified for the broken rule.

This rule of consistency is extremely important and should not be overlooked or bent. Sometimes practitioners develop rather close relationships with the individuals they help and are tempted to bend or break a rule. In the long run this is not a good idea. It may seem somewhat cold, being so firm, direct, and consistent. However, these are just other words for stability, certainty, and calm—emotional situations that an emotionally disturbed individual rarely has experienced. Remember, insta-bility, uncertainty, and inconsistency were the seeds of the indi-vidual's disturbance. It is no favor to break the stability, cer-tainty, and calmness of his or her present environment.

The reader is warned that being consistent with severely disturbed individuals is not as easy as it may seem. Remember, such individuals thrive on inconsistency and, strange as it may seem, may prefer the instability to the stability. This is the environment with which they have learned to cope; even their strange behaviors may be ways of defending against a chaotic, threatening environment. They are defenses used to keep peo-ple away and enhance their self-preservation. A calm, stable, certain environment is unfamiliar and one that requires devel-oping new coping strategies. It must be remembered that emo-tionally disturbed individuals are afraid of change and will strongly resist it. Often, they will unwittingly seduce practitioners into being inconsistent and thus keep things the same. They can become so disruptive that their caretakers will feel that they want to punish them. This very natural feeling has been called *countertransference* by many psychiatrists. The whole issue of countertransference is extremely important and will be discussed shortly.

The difficulty with punishment is that the practitioner is acting inconsistently unless the disturbed individuals are punished all the time. There is a story about a psychiatrist who was so upset about the behavior of the patients on a psychiatric ward of a state hospital that he punished these individuals by giving the entire ward a series of electroshock treatments. Fortunately, that kind of power is illegal; however, physical intervention has been used as a form of punishment. It is hoped that physical intervention is only used as the last resort. To restrain people physically is a breach of their rights as human beings. If physical restraints are being used on a regular basis, something may be dreadfully wrong and those using such methods should be looked at more closely.

Becoming extremely disruptive is one way to seduce practitioners into being inconsistent. Another more subtle way consists of efforts to become the practitioner's friend. This may be accomplished by bringing gifts, giving compliments, doing favors, helping with tasks, and a hundred other little things. To resist such efforts may seem rather cold, yet the practitioner is *not* the client's friend but a professional helper, guide, and teacher. As we have established, it is consistency which will force the client to adopt new ways of behaving, thus bringing about change. By stepping out of the role of professional and treating a client according to another set of rules— that is, inconsistently—the practitioner may in the long run do the client a disservice. Of course, if consistency was the only factor used to help others in need, this would be a cold approach. This is why *all* of the factors in the COUNT system must be used to ensure high-quality care. The next section discusses just how important an optimistic outlook is in helping the emotionally disturbed, but first a few words on the issue of countertransference.

Sigmund Freud (1910) coined the term *countertransference*.

The term essentially is the counterpart of the term *transference*. *Transference* can be defined as the process of grafting onto the practitioner characteristics and relationships associated with the emotions within the client that had been reserved for others in the client's life, such as family members. For example, the client may begin to idolize the practitioner, grow extremely dependent on him or her for assistance and guidance, or even resent and openly criticize the practitioner. It is theorized that such emotions actually are those the individual also has experienced with other significant people in his or her life. It does not take much stretch of the imagination to see that these reactions are the ones a child might have for a parent. In theory, the individual, unconsciously or emotionally, may view the therapist as a parent or other extremely significant person in his or her life. It is not uncommon for individuals to refer to therapists as "Dad" or "Mom" when they are extremely emotionally upset. The transference phenomenon in these cases is very obvious and up front; but even when it is more subtle, it can be seen readily. An individual who is acting in an extremely childish manner, or who gets angry at the practitioner for no apparent reason, may be having transference feelings, transferring the emotional relationship he or she had with a parent or other significant person to the practitioner.

Countertransference is the counterpart of transference. Countertransference comes from the anxiety the individual arouses in the practitioner. That is, the practitioner may begin to see the client as someone he or she is not and may begin to act toward the client as toward other significant people in the practitioner's life. For example, an unreasonable dislike for the individual or an overemotional reaction to the individual's troubles might signal that countertransference is present. This is not to say that whenever a practitioner becomes angry over an individual's behavior, unconscious, unresolved emotional conflicts are at work, but rather that strong emotions, whether positive or negative, should be examined in this light as well as in terms of the present circumstance. One sure way to check whether countertransference is getting in the way is to ask fellow staff members how they feel toward a particular individual. If everyone agrees that John Smith is an incredibly disruptive and disturbing individual, this is not countertransference; John Smith probably is a dislikeable fellow. However, if others see John Smith as all right, while one person has a great dislike for John Smith, countertransference may be present. John Smith may be pulling on something in that person, unconsciously reminding him or her of a parent, an old friend, a mean uncle, or some other significant person. The same would be true if one person had an extreme liking or attraction for an individual and other staff members, at best, were indifferent toward this individual. These are questions you may want to ask your supervisor. All practitioners have unconscious reactions and all experience countertransference reactions to some degree with all clients. Again, it is best to check how other staff members feel toward an individual to see if countertransference is at work.

Once, when I was working at an adult day treatment center, a woman colleague and I were waving goodbye to individuals as they left the program. We suddenly felt like Mom and Dad waving goodbye to the kids. My colleague said that she felt like Ma and Pa Kettle waving goodbye to the children as they left for camp. Countertransference was probably not in effect, although we have found that this feeling of being a parent while working with the emotionally disturbed is quite common, explained in part by their strong transference and dependency needs. In any event, practitioners should not act too much like a parent, but treat clients in a consistently respectful manner.

The issue of countertransference was addressed in order to highlight the need to be aware of one's own feelings toward individuals. Obviously, countertransference can make it extremely difficult to be consistent with an individual. The unfortunate individual will be treated one way by one person and another way by the rest of the staff, potentially forced into the double bind. The individual will get inconsistent double messages that often are extremely confusing and upsetting. The individual in this case is trapped between staff members and not sure what messages to obey and what messages not to obey. In closing, it must be remembered that practitioners not only always must be consistent in their approach in working with an emotionally disturbed individual but the entire staff must work together as a well-tuned, harmonious, consistent unit that can function well and openly.

OPTIMISM

The process whereby people make true what they perceive to be true is called a *self-fulfilling prophecy*. If I believe that I am a "slow learner," I will act as though I am a slow learner. In an experiment designed to test this theory of the self-fulfilling prophecy (Rosenthal & Jacobson, 1968), teachers in a public elementary school were told that several of their students were "rapid bloomers." In fact, these "special" children were chosen at random and were not necessarily rapid bloomers. The researchers discovered that students who were expected to bloom showed significantly more improvement in IQ scores than did those students for whom no expectations were held. These children were victims, or in this case, beneficiaries, of their teachers' self-fulfilling prophecies. The way in which these children were perceived by others may have influenced the way in which the children perceived themselves. In other words, the way in which people perceive themselves has a dramatic influence on their behavior.

Goldstein (1962) found that therapists who expect no improvement tend to have patients who do not improve, while therapists who expect their patients to improve tend to have patients who do improve. Being optimistic does not mean denying to the individual the seriousness of his or her problem or the amount of time and effort it will take to induce change. Being optimistic means being honest both with ourselves and with the individual about the seriousness of the problem, yet continuing to work even though there is no rapid or immediate change and the work, at times, is very frustrating. If, over time, the individual sees that the practitioner is a strong, optimistic person who will not be overwhelmed or deterred by the magnitude of the client's problems, change is very likely to occur. If the individual sees that someone is committed to him or her and that person continues to have a very strong, optimistic outlook on life and the future, it is very difficult for this individual not to change. An emotionally disturbed individual has experienced a lifetime of poor self-fulfilling prophecies, announcing that, "My life is no good," "I will never amount to anything," "I am schizophrenic, and schizophrenics never get better." If the individual is offered hope, this, in itself, begins to change the individual's self-perceptions. Gradually, self-fulfilling prophecies such as "My life is OK," "I can amount to something," and "Schizophrenics do get better," begin to take hold.

However, the individual should never be allowed to think that the work is going to be quick and easy; this would only lead to another failure. The emotionally disturbed individual has gone through a lifetime of mistrust, hopelessness, and pain to reach this point in time; he or she will not get better overnight. This message should be communicated to the individual along with a powerful message of hope and optimism. Improvement in the individual's condition is likely to occur if the individual is willing to work very hard. At some point during the development of a relationship with an emotionally disturbed individual, this message of hope and hard work should be discussed. An optimistic, positive outlook is a powerful tool in bringing about change.

With these insights in mind, consider what a positive, optimistic, hopeful outlook could do for an emotionally disturbed individual's self-perception. Ronald Laing questions the extent to which schizophrenic behavior is self-fulfilling. The following experiment is proposed:

Experiment: Take a group of normal persons, group N (by agreed criteria)
Treat them as schizophrenic
Take a group of "early" schizophrenics, group X (by agreed criteria)
Treat them as normal

Prediction: Many of N will begin to display the agreed criteria of schizophrenia
Many of X will begin to display the agreed criteria of normality

Experiment: Take a group of "early" schizophrenics
(i) treat them in role as crazy
(ii) treat them like oneself as sane

Prediction: In (i) the "symptomatology" of schizophrenia will be
very much greater
(ii) the symptomatology of schizophrenia will be greatly dimin-
ished. (Laing, 1972, pp. 46–47)

The instillation of hope is valuable not only for severely
disturbed individuals but, as one would imagine, for everyone.
We all like to feel that tomorrow will be a better day and that
there is hope for the future. However, the emotionally disturbed
individual will have a more difficult time believing this. Everyone likes to be around people who are positive, optimistic, and
radiate energy. Irvin Yalom (1983) has indicated that the instillation of hope is one of the most important factors in being
therapeutically effective. Consider the effectiveness of faith healing. An individual's physical and/or emotional difficulties can be
helped if one puts enough faith in the healer's ability to cure.
There is a massive amount of data documenting the effectiveness of faith healing, placebo treatment, and treatment mediated entirely through hope and conviction. Consider the practice of witchcraft, voodooism in particular. In societies where
voodooism is practiced regularly, the individuals truly believe in
the power of the witch doctor. The witch doctor essentially is a
professional worker of magic, who in primitive societies often
works to cure sickness. Much of the witch doctor's success is
attributed to the sick individual's unwavering belief in the power
of the sorcerer's spell. The self-fulfilling prophecy of "I will get
better" or "I will get worse" is planted in the mind of the individual by the witch doctor. We have all heard the stories of people
dying from a voodoo curse. It is highly probable that if an individual's belief that "I will die" is powerful enough, this prophecy, in
fact, may come true. Of course, the opposite belief, "I will live,"
may also become self-fulfilling.

Historically, individuals who have suffered from extreme
disturbances of emotion have always been looked upon as incurable, hopeless, or, at best, as having a horrible burden to carry

throughout life. Such self-fulfilling prophecies have not helped these individuals gain a better understanding of themselves or made their lives more pleasant. Even today many professionals, including administrators, psychiatrists, social workers, and psychologists still see the severely emotionally disturbed individual as incurable. There are many treatment settings where the unwritten rule is that "no one gets better around here." If the administrators, psychiatrists, social workers, and psychologists all believe that "no one gets better around here," how long do you think it takes the "patients" to follow this rule. The emotionally disturbed individual is very difficult to reach on a therapeutic level. However, if one consistently maintains an optimistic outlook and continues working with this individual to the best of one's ability, the odds are very strong that the individual will improve.

This section has tried to show the importance of an optimistic outlook in working with the emotionally disturbed. Many emotionally disturbed individuals have experienced a lifetime of following negative self-fulfilling prophecies. They continually see themselves as losers, as no good, and as hopeless. It is the job of the worker to inspire and change these negative self-concepts. Of course, *one should not push the individual or encourage false hope,* for this will only be setting the individual up for another failure. What is needed is a realistic belief in the potential goodness of human nature, a positive outlook on life and on the future, and the ability to see beauty in even the smallest and most insignificant things: in short, being optimistic. Such an optimistic outlook is contagious and eventually will tempt the emotionally disturbed individual away from his or her withdrawn disillusionment. The emotionally disturbed individual is desperate to find some meaning in his or her chaotic life, and when this despair is challenged by showing that life can be meaningful and worth living, much has been accomplished. Optimism, a feeling of hope, and a sense of meaning all are qualities rare to an emotionally disturbed individual. The next section shows that being consistent and optimistic are not the only factors needed while working with emotionally disturbed individuals; an unbiased attitude toward those who seek help also is important.

UNBIASED ATTITUDE

The choice of one's career or profession should be made with a good knowledge of the kind of people with whom one will work. For example, if I were to choose to become an auto mechanic, I would expect to work with all sectors of the public but I know I would spend most of my working hours with engines and cars. On the other hand, if I chose to be a legal secretary, I would imagine most of my working hours would be spent in an office with middle-class professionals. Now, in choosing the field of mental health, I expect to spend most of my working hours with a variety of people. Every day I could expect to be working closely with psychiatrists, psychologists, social workers, counselors, occupational and recreational therapists, nurses, teachers, and a variety of other practitioners. In addition, the patients or clients at the facility could be of any age, sex, race, religion; they could be rich, poor, middle-class, or on welfare; and they could be good looking, ugly, fat, skinny, tall, or short. Furthermore, the emotional disturbances that the individuals exhibit could range from mild to extremely disturbed.

Being unbiased means being free from all prejudice and favoritism. First, it is hoped that one would not discriminate against an individual because he or she is emotionally disturbed. Second, and equally important, it is hoped that one would not discriminate against an individual because of age, sex, race, religion, socioeconomic class, or personal attributes. Those who discriminate against a group of people because of some characteristic do not belong in the field of mental health. They cannot be helpful to emotionally disturbed individuals if they are held back by their own prejudices. Of course, to one degree or another, all people probably carry around a certain amount of prejudice, for the very fact that people are most likely to be attracted to others who appear to be similar to themselves. Prejudice involves prejudgments that cause people to act in certain ways toward members of a particular group. For example, let us assume that I am prejudiced against those with dirty ears. I assume that "those people" who have "those ears" must not have good hygiene skills, have a poor level of aspiration, and because of this, they also must have low intelligence levels. "Those people" are not too bright and probably will never change.

If I had this prejudice, how could I possibly work effectively with one of "those people"? My prejudice would interfere with my ability to help this individual. I would be doing this individual a disservice if I tried to pretend I did not have this prejudice. I would have to put on a phony front of acceptance that would be unnatural and dishonest. Prejudices are very powerful factors within one's personality but they can be overcome through education and intergroup contact.

Favoritism is like prejudice, but instead of discriminating against a certain group, that group is favored. For example, if I like "those with dirty ears," or, better still, if I have "dirty ears," I would probably favor "those with dirty ears." I may bend some rules for them, or even take them under my wing. As we have seen throughout this chapter, such conditions are not therapeutic. Countertransference, pessimism, prejudice, and inconsistency impede any progress that could be made in working with an emotionally disturbed individual. Establishing a trusting relationship with an emotionally disturbed individual is likely to fail if issues of the individual's subculture are ignored or discriminated against.

An unbiased approach in working with the emotionally disturbed, in other words, is a humane approach. One cannot be therapeutically effective and still discriminate against the individual one is trying to help; it just does not work. This section has tried to show that any form of prejudice or favoritism can be destructive in forming a therapeutic alliance with an emotionally disturbed individual. Employment in the field of mental health gives one an opportunity for personal growth and enrichment. It is a people-oriented field and requires working closely with people from all walks of life. We have found that an unbiased attitude, optimism, and consistency all are qualities necessary to encourage a frightened, confused, and isolated individual away from such disturbing behavior. It is hoped that all those who choose to work in this social profession have an unbiased attitude toward people in general. In our next section we will discuss just how important it is to be natural, to be oneself, while establishing a trusting relationship with an emotionally disturbed individual.

NATURALNESS

Being natural simply means being oneself rather than trying to be something one is not. Individuals suffering from emotional disturbances, for the most part, are very sensitive individuals and generally "pick up" on subtle interpersonal cues. Because they are terrified of their environment they want to know as much as possible about the world that surrounds them so they can protect themselves from it.

I once worked with Paul, an individual labeled *paranoid schizophrenic*. Paul was an expert at reading people's faces for emotion. He knew when I was anxious, depressed, happy, or experiencing whatever emotion. In the development of our relationship, he would always take great pleasure in pointing out whenever I was feeling anxious. This, of course, would only increase my anxious feelings. Paul needed to feel that he was in control and, to accomplish this, would zero in on my faults and weaknesses. Paul was a perceptive, sensitive young man; however, he often used this ability as a defense to keep himself isolated from people. For example, a colleague of mine met Paul for only five minutes. During this meeting Paul made a rather large joke over the fact that one of my colleague's ears was shorter than the other. My colleague was naturally upset and embarrassed by this episode, although Paul was quite pleased and teased him throughout the meeting. What was striking about this was that I had known my colleague for almost two years and I never noticed that one of his ears was shorter than the other!

The moral of this story is that emotionally disturbed individuals, for the most part, are perceptive, sensitive individuals. The people who choose to work in this field not only need to know themselves well, but they will have to be honest with themselves and others. As stated earlier, they must be themselves, be natural, and not try to be something they are not; otherwise they are being phony. Of course, it is difficult to ascertain exactly what being natural is, because people tend to assume many different roles depending on the situation they are in. For example, one's behavior would be different at a formal dinner entertaining some dignified guests than at a football game. People tend to "act," and thus behave in a slightly or, in some cases, a greatly different manner depending on the circumstances.

At work, people tend to act somewhat differently than at home. This is not to say that one is "phony" at work and "real" at home. It only means that different situations require different behaviors. Theorists often refer to this behavior as a social role: that is, a pattern of behavior expected by both oneself and others from the person occupying a particular position in a social situation. Rules, called *norms,* provide a standard of action that specifies what behavior is normal, or expected, and what behavior is abnormal. So while at a football game my social role is that of football fan; I am allowed to yell and scream at this social occasion because the norms or rules of behavior specify that yelling is normal and expected in this social situation. A different social role and a different set of norms would apply at a formal dinner.

When we are working with an individual who has some emotional difficulties, practitioners assume a work role. But this work role must be natural, a role in which they feel comfortable. Each person needs a variation on the work role that suits his or her personality and view of the job. An outgoing, happy-go-lucky type of person will seem phony in a very serious, dignified role. On the other hand, a very serious individual will find it unnatural to try to be a happy-go-lucky individual. Yet, each of these persons has something special and real to offer the emotionally disturbed individual, the natural optimism of the happy-go-lucky person and the natural respect for the individual's struggle of the serious person. Honesty always is the best policy while working with the emotionally disturbed. Lying to an emotionally disturbed individual is inconsistent, and as already has been explained, being inconsistent is not being helpful. Being honest means never having to remember what you did or said in the past. Honesty in both your behavior and words does a tremendous service to oneself and others. Being phony does not work, being oneself does—being natural.

TRUSTWORTHINESS

Consistency, optimism, an unbiased attitude, and naturalness all are qualities that can be observed within oneself and that can be continually improved upon. The issue of trustworthiness is a totally different matter. Theoretically, one can force oneself into being consistent, optimistic, unbiased, and even natural; however, one cannot force trust from another person. Trust is something that develops over time, and trust can be obtained only over time. For example, I am sure you would have a deeper sense of trust toward someone with whom you have had a close relationship for over ten years than someone you have known only for a few weeks. Trust is something that develops. It is the most important quality that can develop while working with an emotionally disturbed individual. If, while working with an emotionally disturbed individual you sense that this individual is beginning to trust you, you have done an incredibly brilliant job! You may be the only person in this individual's life that he or she can trust. In fact, you may be the only person this individual has ever trusted. But you cannot force a person to trust you; it is really his or her decision. A rule of thumb is that the more disturbed an individual is, the longer it will take this individual to trust you. It is not uncommon that in some cases it may take several years before the individual can trust you. Some individuals may never develop a basic sense of trust.

Erickson (1950) describes how people learn to trust the world around them. He maintains that the development of basic trust is established during the first year of life, during which the child is completely dependent upon the parent. The child needs to be taken care of, needs to be fed, dressed, to have diapers changed, to be talked to, to be bathed, to be hugged, and a host of other things. The parent responds to all of the child's needs and attempts to satisfy them. Erickson maintains that basic trust of the world or, on the other hand, mistrust of the world develops during the first year of life. Theoretically, if all the child's needs are met, the child begins to see the world as a safe, trustworthy place. If, on the other hand, the child's needs are not met or if the child is actually abused or neglected during this time, the child begins to see the world as unsafe and cold. It is hypothesized that the severely emotionally disturbed individual has not had the chance to learn this attitude of basic trust. There are theories to suggest that the child's needs were not met during the first year of life, which began this gradual development of mistrust of the world. It also is theorized that the individual who was to later develop a severe emotional disturbance was never given the opportunity to develop trust throughout the childhood years. Recall the double-bind hypothesis; with these insights in mind, it is no wonder that the emotionally disturbed individual is frightened of people, terrified of the world, and unable to trust the environment.

It is the practitioner's job to help these unfortunate individuals begin to feel somewhat secure about the world around them. If a secure feeling can be obtained, these individuals may begin to trust the surrounding world and may no longer need to withdraw or act bizarre to keep people away, to bend reality to defend against a hostile world. This individual, having learned to trust, will no longer need to be an isolated individual, but just another person living, loving, growing, and experiencing the wonders of life.

This chapter described the conditions and attitudes necessary to work most effectively with the emotionally disturbed individual. The COUNT system forces people to look at their own emotions, attitudes, and beliefs. Only by looking inward and knowing oneself well can a practitioner be most effective while working with the emotionally disturbed. The more in touch the practitioner is with his or her feelings, the more that person can help others get in touch with their feelings. Emotionally disturbed individuals are desperate in trying to understand their own feelings.

The confusion, bizarre behavior, hallucinations, social withdrawal, and delusions are ways the disturbed individual has found to cope with and adapt to his or her environment. It is the practitioner's job to tempt the disturbed individual away from withdrawn disillusionment and to show that life can be meaningful and worth living. The best way to go about this is to try and develop a basic sense of trust within the individual. The COUNT system is designed to help the emotionally disturbed individual begin to feel somewhat secure about the world. A consistent, optimistic, unbiased, and natural approach is necessary in beginning to establish a secure environment. If a secure environment can be obtained, it is very possible that the emotionally disturbed individual may begin to trust the world. A basic sense of trust is the key to human happiness, growth, love, sharing, sacrifice, commitment, and caring. It is only through these ideals that life is given a sense of meaning and understanding. To see a once broken human being develop and blossom into a caring, loving, and trusting person is a sight truly worth waiting for.

7. *We're All in This Together*
Group Therapy

When one considers the issue of facilitating group therapy with the severely emotionally disturbed, it becomes apparent that there are few established guidelines. In fact, the professional sources have indicated that treatment of this population in a group setting is difficult (Yalom 1983).

Nevertheless, whether by desire or design, practitioners sometimes are forced into group treatment approaches. The reasons vary, from scarce resources to economic conditions to treatment rationale. Whatever the reason, group therapy is a common method for treating the severely emotionally disturbed.

WHY GROUPS?

Groups are formed, at least in part, to reflect people's efforts to be united with others and to decrease their feelings of alienation and isolation. Uniting in groups enhances one's efforts to be accepted by others and gain a sense of self-worth and belonging. When treating the emotionally disturbed in groups, feelings of isolation and inadequacy in the areas of interpersonal relationships are the main obstacles to overcome.

The uniting thread that holds the social fabric of all people together is communication. Our effectiveness in relating to one another is a function of our ability to convey certain ideas and impressions to others. Assisting the emotionally disturbed in developing interpersonal communication skills will decrease their feelings of alienation and help the person find the common bond with humanity that unites people into one group or another.

Most emotionally disturbed individuals realize, whether they admit it or not, that they have a communication problem. Usually, by the time a practitioner sees these individuals, they have reached a point of self-isolation or have been alienated by others. They have strained their interpersonal relationships to the breaking point and have been abandoned by their families, friends, and almost everyone else. Emotionally disturbed individuals seem to be aware that they think differently, act differently, and experience life differently, and are shaken to the very roots of their existence.

Messages from the environment are confusing and quite often place these individuals in a "double bind" or "no win situation." No one else seems to understand what they are experiencing. As a result, these individuals drift deeper into their delusionary worlds, which protect them from the unpredictable real world. But one message does get through: They are alone! A practitioner perhaps will provide their only outside relationship. They have been abandoned by everyone else, either by their own rejection of the world or by the inability or unwillingness of others to understand them. Emotionally disturbed individuals are alone and afraid. Some are trapped in a world of terrifying delusions; others hear voices telling them to do bizarre things that are confusing and frightening.

In one case, an emotionally disturbed woman climbed up on the cross of a church and attempted to remove Jesus, crying out that Jesus had asked her to get him down. Her hands were bleeding as she clawed desperately at the stone figure. In a few hours she too turned to stone, catatonic, so frightened and overwhelmed with fear that she could not move.

Reflect for a moment on a terrifying dream you might have had, so terrifying that you could not scream and your legs could not move. This response goes beyond the escape response of fight or flight. This immobility seems to be the final instinctual response to fear in an effort to protect one's life. Standing there frozen, the individual hopes that the terrifying threat will go away long enough for there to be one last chance to escape.

This final response to fear has been documented in animal studies by Ratner (1967; 1975), which seems to indicate that this response may be instinctual by nature. "Moreover, despite the animals' trance-like or stuporous appearance, the animals are characterized by a rapid heartbeat, until just before termination of the immobility. . . . The adaptive significance of this response in animals is that it is the last stage of defense of a prey under attack by a predator." Karon speculates regarding these studies that "Some of these responses tend to save the life of the individual, and other responses tend to preserve the lives of other members of the species. Both types of responses would obviously be selected for by evolution" (Karon and Vandenbos 1981, pp. 47–52). Considering this type of response in animals may offer some insight as to what the catatonic individual may be experiencing. The individual described earlier was so terrified by her own behavior and thoughts that her overwhelming fear put her in a catatonic state.

One possible way to effectively help someone in this type of condition is through building a trusting relationship with the person and gradually increasing the person's social contact by using group therapy sessions. A group can provide a safe structured environment, consistency, and support. Groups provide their members with the opportunity to communicate to others with similar problems and experiences. In addition, groups provide a setting where people can safely address their concerns and develop trust, which is essential for normalization back into the community. The formation of this community of peers, a family of isolated members to support one another, is perhaps the deepest reason for the birth of a group.

GROUP DYNAMICS

The immature person cannot permit himself to understand the world of another because it is different from his own and therefore threatening to him. Only the individual who is reasonably secure in his own identity and selfhood can permit the other person to be different, unique, and can understand and appreciate the uniqueness. (Rogers, 1983, p. 192)

The most basic question of any individual in a group is Will I be accepted? This is particularly important to disturbed individuals because of their fears of isolation and alienation as well as a fear of close personal intimacy. In addition, they fear the feeling of engulfment or being swallowed up by others followed by their rejection of them as a person. Therefore, promoting a positive and safe atmosphere within the group, through an air of genuine caring and respect for each individual's contribution, is a key element. Establishing trust among group members is the goal of the group therapy process. Fostering trust is accomplished by the acceptance of each individual for who he or she is as a person.

Since the group may be composed of a constellation of individuals with different functioning levels, ages, symptoms, and backgrounds, the leader should prepare for the inevitable problems. Some group members may be disruptive or act out behaviorally. Others may experience some major life crises during the group session that require immediate and individual attention. Unfortunately, the group leader does not have control over all these variables but simply has to do his or her best to work with the situation. Some of these problems will emerge, at one time or another, for all group facilitators. Problem solving and crisis resolution are the nature of work with the emotionally disturbed individual.

When working in a group setting with extremely difficult individuals, it can be very hard to keep everyone's attention. Group activities require close contact with others, which may be anxiety provoking and stressful for some. Each individual's tolerance level of stress will vary, even when exposed to the same situation. It is not unusual for some individuals to remain aloof and not become directly involved in the group discussion while others wander off. These individuals may keep themselves on the fringe of the group, but they still are involved. Always encourage and support the group members' involvement in the group task, at whatever level. Each one of these behaviors will need special attention. While being supportive, request their input, and value whatever contributions they make.

Sometimes, a person will require individual attention before being able to reenter the group. Therefore, it is important to have established an open and trusting relationship with the person. Developing this relationship is the first goal of any group leader. In this way, the leader maintains contact with the wandering person, whose problem may be related to the ability to follow the task, level of attention, boredom, or perhaps the ability to cope with the stimulation of the group. Emotionally disturbed individuals may need some space to decrease their anxiety. One way a program can promise "space" is by establishing a lounge. These lounge areas can be set up to decrease the overall stimulation of the group for the individual.

Maintaining consistency is an important aspect for the reentry of the wandering individual back into the group. A group scheduled at the same time, place, and with the same group leader will provide a stable reentry point for the wandering individual. The wandering individual wants to belong but is afraid, approaching and avoiding the stressful situation of group interaction. If the group remains safe, stable, and consistent, the wandering individual will approach the group again, when ready. Knowing what to expect and what is expected from them will help the group members decrease their stress.

Norms or Rules

Establishing norms is another important function of group dynamics. Norms or rules assist the group in determining what is to be expected and set the groundwork for building trust and safety. There may be norms on attendance or on the content of materials given to the group; that is, not to come late. Norms may determine the length of time that someone may speak, how another should listen, or whether each person is responsible for what he or she says or does.

Accepting responsibility for what one says, does, thinks, or feels is called *taking ownership*. In certain groups, there are extensive rules for ownership. A group member who says, "I can't do something," is asked to try substituting the words *I won't do something*. The perspective of the statement changes dramatically. The rule proposed to the group is that the words *I can't* involve only a physical impossibility, that is, a man *can't* have a baby. Another substitution involves changing why questions to how questions. This opens up the possibility for an actual answer. For example, "How did something happen?" is different and more possible to answer than "Why did something happen?" Changing the words "I feel guilty" to "I resent" will give the individual an insight into some of his or her feelings and thoughts about his or her problems (Perls, 1967, pp. 12–48). These counseling cues have been used for years in group sessions and are extremely powerful statements that are not appropriate for all groups. The many different types of therapeutic groups will not be explored here, except to provide some ideas of how extensive group norms and rules can be.

Just as there are norms for ownership, there are norms for feedback. Feedback is the ability to respond, assist, and learn from one another. It is a true reflection of the ability to understand what has been said. Everyone wants feedback, for this confirms one's existence. The interaction provides a sense of involvement, belonging, clarification, and reinforcement. Whether positive or negative, feedback tells people something about themselves. Feedback can confirm their impressions of the world or dispel them. It can expand their awareness of who they are and influence their values. All people receive signals and responses from everyone and everything they touch in life. These responses all help them define the world they live in and who they are as people. The whole ability to learn from life takes the form of feedback. Fairness and consistency in the enforcement of the group norms will promote an atmosphere of trust. Everyone should feel safe and accepted in the group, as this is the most basic premise in any group formation.

In groups, the individual has a unique opportunity to try out new behaviors and receive objective feedback from others. For example, have you ever found yourself imitating another person? Children begin imitating their parents, adopting their behaviors and values, but over time they acquire new behaviors and values from their experiences. As a result of this process, they end by defining themselves somewhat differently than before. People always try out new behaviors and perspectives based upon their adaptation to the world around them. This is

all part of finding out who they are and what feels comfortable
for them as people.

GROUP COMPOSITION

> The more often people get together, the more they interact. The
> more that people interact, the more they like each other. The
> more that people like each other, the more they interact. (Homans, 1950, pp. 112–113)

The composition of groups seems to be as important as how
groups are conducted. Determining the needs of each individual and whether he or she can benefit from working in a group
setting is the first objective in establishing the group composition. Just as there are a large variety of individual problems,
there are a variety of groups and group activities. The first, and
most renowned, is the classical group therapy session. An immense amount of information is available on therapy groups,
ranging in scope and nature from psychoanalytic, gestalt, or
client-centered therapeutic approaches to sensitivity and assertiveness training. Such groups generally are led by therapists
with years of professional training and experience in the field.

Practitioners just entering the field are more likely to conduct groups with more limited objectives. Such groups may be
used to develop skills in the areas of vocational training, advanced daily living skills, educational advancement, and community awareness, depending on the needs of the group members.

Suppose, for example, the following individuals were assigned randomly to your care. They have a variety of needs,
and the center for which you work decided that they possibly
could benefit from a group setting. You have been handed a list
of individuals, with little or no background information on
them. What types of groups would you form based upon their
individual needs?

Mark is a 22-year-old white man who arrives at the first
group meeting dressed in a full-length robe, smoking a cigarette. The smoke curls above his head. He introduces himself

as Christ and claims that the only way the world can be saved is if everyone else got off.

Bill is a 33-year-old white man with a long history of hospitalizations, involving twenty-one admissions since the age of 15. He has a college education and grew up in an upper-class neighborhood. He mumbles for a moment and introduces himself as China.

Martha is a 56-year-old black woman who has been married for twenty years. She looks disheveled, with her hair uncombed, and appears very emotionally strained. She claims that other individuals are substituting their deformed body parts for hers by a process of mental shocks.

Mary is a 26-year-old white woman of limited intelligence. She wants to complete her general educational degree and go to work. She grew up in a poor family and was placed in foster care at the age of 10. She has attempted suicide a number of times in the recent past.

Fred is a 55-year-old Hispanic man who owned a business at one time. Recently he was released into the community after twenty years in institutions. He has the skills to work but no longer is motivated to work. Fred feels there is nothing to live for and he has no goals for the future.

Mike is a 28-year-old white man who is taking college courses in drafting. He has been having difficulty controlling his impulses and often he will become very angry and destroy things.

Bob is a 29-year-old black man with epilepsy and a limited intelligence. He wants to be independent and live alone, yet can not take care of his basic needs of food, clothing, and shelter.

As you may have noticed, this group contains a wide variety of people and problems. Often, group leaders have little or no control over selecting the mixture of individuals in the group. Because of economic factors or limited resources, groups may not be broken down by considerations of IQ, economic status, age, or similar characteristics, even though these factors play an important role in group formation and cohesiveness. *Cohesiveness* is how close the group members feel toward one another. When possible, members should be matched by similar characteristics. These similarities have been proven to be factors in having a successful and fruitful group.

There are numerous disadvantages to conducting groups with members who have dissimilar characteristics (Yalom, 1975):

1. The group dropout rate is higher.
2. There is an increase in disruptiveness.
3. Some members find it difficult to concentrate on the group task.

The purpose of your group is to address some of the major life problems these individuals have endured. There are countless problems either created as a consequence of their illnesses or as symptoms of it. They range in scope and intensity from taking care of themselves physically to rebuilding identities with high self-esteem and a normal life-style.

It is important to assess your group members. Each group member has individual needs and represents a different level of functioning. Review each case record carefully, talk with your colleagues, and become familiar with the individuals you are helping. Usually, from assessing their background information you will be able to determine the overall functioning level of each individual. *Functioning level* indicates where an individual is on the continuum of skill development leading to independence, for example, can prepare meals, plan for the future, find a job, and so on. In determining the overall levels of functioning, you may want to find out whether the person currently is having some major problem taking care of his or her basic needs (food, clothing, and shelter) or faces only a minimal amount of discomfort and interference in daily life. Between these two extremes, there are hundreds, if not thousands, of skills to develop. Group composition is based upon similar functioning levels as well as similar diagnoses. Although grouping individuals by similar characteristics as mentioned previously is important, grouping individuals by their functioning level is imperative.

Sometimes the problems seem overwhelming and impossible to solve, especially when examined in their entirety. Generally, these individuals tend to look at their difficulties all at once and experience a feeling of futility. They need to assess their problems, viewing them in terms of smaller, more manageable, and thus solvable, problems. In breaking down these problems the group members will need assistance in ranking each problem by its importance relative to eventual independence. Through the assessment process, you will learn each individual's strengths and weaknesses. By concentrating on strengths, you will more effectively teach developmental skills and increase the ability to complete tasks successfully.

After the initial assessment and identification of the individual's problems, the following exercise may be one way you can get the ball rolling in a group. Have the group members write down each specific problem or concern they may have. Although all the problems are of importance, determining a starting point based upon the most important skills to develop is useful. Next, have each person put an *A* next to the most immediate and important problems to solve, then place a *B* next to the problems that need to be addressed as soon as possible. Finally, have them place a *C* next to the problems that are not creating difficulty for them right now.

WHERE TO FROM HERE?

The assessment process should help determine where each individual's problem areas lie. From these can be developed a comprehensive list of goals or skills areas to be worked on within the group. Some goals or skills may have to be addressed individually, whereas others can be generalized to an entire group activity. In either case, the skills to be developed must first be broken down into still smaller steps, each moving progressively toward the goal. These subgoals or subobjectives should be observable and measurable. Goals and objectives may be measured by the number of prompts required to elicit the behavior, by the time it takes to accomplish something, and so forth.

Progress is easier to determine if you have measured the frequency of the target behavior or symptoms prior to treatment. This is called *determining a baseline.* Baseline measurement is useful, prior to any type of treatment. Whether a behavior is to be changed or a skill to be developed, knowing how often the behavior occurs naturally is useful.

For instance, Warren lets out a bloodcurdling scream twelve times a day. Initially, Sandra, the practitioner, may want to radically decrease the screaming, which she determined was an attempt to get staff's attention. Sandra cannot eliminate this behavior without replacing it with something more appropriate. By determining Warren's needs, she can teach him more socially appropriate ways of attracting attention while at the same time ignoring the screaming.

The effectiveness of the treatment plan can be evaluated at each point or measurable objective along the way. Such measurements allow practitioners to quickly determine if an approach is effective and reevaluate the treatment approach.

In setting goals for an individual, try to phrase them in a positive, constructive way. For example, to eliminate Warren's screaming, Sandra could negatively phrase the goal as "Stop screaming." Instead, she wants to focus on appropriate social skills for gaining attention from others. By attempting to turn a negative goal into a positive one, she clarifies the end results she wants to achieve. Phrasing goals positively will take some practice, but it is a constructive way to approach a treatment strategy. In the example of Warren's screaming, Sandra could state the goal more positively, by focusing on appropriate behaviors to obtain attention from others, such as "Increase hand raising to obtain attention."

The treatment plan is the process by which goals are established to help with the individual's problems and concerns. There will be times when an individual progresses rapidly through the therapeutic treatment plan until a certain point, then suddenly begins to fail and even starts regressing. In this instance, failure may indicate something internally or externally is interfering with the individual's progress. The first response to this failure would be an attempt to determine its immediate cause. Perhaps the treatment plan should be reexamined and simplified into smaller, more manageable steps. Both success and failure will be part of the group leader's experiences. People learn from both experiences; failures may be just as enlightening as successes.

As the group member moves through each progressive step of the treatment plan, it is important to make the steps simple enough for the person to achieve them with success. Meeting a new challenge with success gives one the confidence to accept more risks, enhances one's self-esteem, and improves one's overall attitude toward life. Motivation also increases with a higher self-esteem, increased confidence, and an improved attitude, enabling the person to achieve the progressively more difficult steps toward the desired goal.

Success is reinforcing. Everyone wants and needs positive reinforcement, although emotionally disturbed individuals have probably met with more failure than success most of their lives. Through positive reinforcement, they gain the strength and courage to accept more challenges and risks in order to move ahead toward independence. As each new skill is developed, you will be witness to the ego building process of individualization. They begin to have more faith in themselves and make decisions for what goals they want to reach in their lives.

Successful achievement of goals is essential in treatment. In order to ensure success, the group leader should monitor the steps taken by the individual. For example, if three attempts at a particular step have been unsuccessful for the individual, perhaps those steps need to be broken down even further. This may seem very difficult, but successful results will pay off in the long run.

Reinforcement plays a big part in the success of any treatment plan. Each person responds to reinforcement, whether consciously or unconsciously. For example, people go to work each day for various reasons that are reinforcing to them in some way (e.g., fulfillment, money, self-esteem).

Reinforcers provide motivation, confidence, and security. The emotionally disturbed individual also is reinforced and motivated by achieving something he or she wants. Self-identified reinforcers commonly are used in treatment plans to reward the individual for the successful completion of a goal. Reinforcers are broken down into two types. The first, primary reinforcers, can be anything that is concrete and tangible (e.g., apple,

M&Ms, pop, or cigarette). It would be uncommon to use these types of reinforcers with the emotionally disturbed. The second type of reinforcer, praise, should be given whether a primary reinforcer is given or not. For example, someone who does a good job should be praised for how well he or she did. Praise can go a long way as a reinforcer to improve one's self-esteem and sense of self-worth. It also develops motivation to obtain more recognition. This type of secondary reinforcer has proven to be the most effective type with the emotionally disturbed.

Emotionally disturbed individuals already have a wealth of skills. Sometimes, they lack the motivation to use these skills, and a plan is needed to provide motivation. Experiencing consistent consequences for their actions and decisions in a structured way provides external support that encourages internal control for their actions. The term *structure* simply means setting normal, consistent, realistic limits for the individual. Providing structure makes the world more predictable and less frightening for the disturbed person. It also gives them a sense that someone cares for them and is in control even if they feel out of control. As mentioned earlier, consequences can be positive, but they can also be negative or even punishing. It is the philosophy of this book to be positive in order to produce change and increase skill development; therefore, punishment and negative reinforcement will not be addressed.

As practitioners work in groups and with treatment plans, they find that certain things work and others do not. Remember what did not work, but write down what did work effectively, thus developing a treatment resource file. These treatment plans and procedures can be referred to should similar cases or problems arise in the future. Although all people are different and each plan should be individualized, this resource file will provide some effective guidelines and perhaps save some time in reaching goals.

HOW TO GENERATE NEW IDEAS

It is important for the group leader to continue generating ideas, activities, and goals for the group. However, even the best group leaders will reach their limits and feel that they have exhausted every possible idea or activity. These suggestions may help in resolving this common dilemma.

1. Attend conferences or seminars. They are excellent opportunities for obtaining new ideas; in addition, they provide an opportunity to break away from of one's everyday situation and refresh oneself.
2. Talk with colleagues within the program and staff members from other programs. This is another way to share ideas and activities, perhaps, through monthly meetings at rotating sites. Doing this will give you an opportunity to see how others operate and conduct groups.
3. Keep informed of available resources by reading, talking, and listening to others.
4. Reflect upon the main goal of the program. This helps one stay centered and keep on course. For example, if the main goal is eventual independence into the community, then every effort and activity needs to be a direct step leading to this goal.
5. Set up a brainstorming session with colleagues. This technique helps get a group warmed up and creates new ideas through primary and secondary associative processes.

There are some basic guidelines to follow for a brainstorming session:

1. Limit brainstorming sessions to 3 minutes.
2. Every idea is okay; encourage group members to say the first thing that comes to their minds.
3. Do not evaluate ideas until after the session. Evaluating or being critical of ideas during the brainstorming session may limit creativity.
4. It is okay to add to or free-associate with other's ideas.
5. Appoint one person to write down all ideas. Later the brainstorming group can evaluate and rank the suggestions, while assessing their feasibility.

As a warm-up exercise, begin the brainstorming session by thinking of all the different ways to use a piece of rope, then continue with all the different types of activities that can be

done in the group program. Chances are enough new ideas will
be suggested to last a year!

ADVANCED DAILY LIVING SKILLS

When considering activities for the group, addressing individuals' basic needs takes precedence. These needs, known as
advanced daily living (ADL) *skills,* concentrate on developing
skills in the areas of feeding oneself, getting dressed, acquiring
shelter, and taking care of personal hygiene. Without these
most basic skills, movement back into the community for the
emotionally disturbed individual becomes impossible. One
may need assistance in determining such things as dressing appropriately for the weather conditions, eating a balanced diet,
finding housing, and maintaining one's home. In addition, each
skill can be used as an activity in a group setting.

To get some ideas of the different types of ADL skills,
consider the usual daily activities most people engage in; for
example, cooking, cleaning, maintenance, bathing. After assessing the individual's needs and determining which skills
need building (say, toothbrushing), then examine all the steps
required for you to accomplish this task. For example, in brush-
ing teeth, the person

1. Picks up the toothpaste,
2. Takes off the cap,
3. Picks up the toothbrush,
4. Squeezes toothpaste onto the toothbrush,
5. Turns on the faucet,
6. Raises the brush to his or her teeth,
7. Brushes the top teeth, brushes the bottom teeth,
8. Brushes the back and side teeth,
9. Rinses his or her mouth,
10. Rinses his or her toothbrush,
11. Turns off the faucet,
12. Puts things away.

This example was included to demonstrate just how complex a relatively simple task can be. Each task of daily living

can be broken down into discrete, achievable steps. The following list presents skills that can be applied as goals toward independence in advanced daily living skills groups:

Personal hygiene	Maintaining yard
Grooming	Bathing or taking showers
Wearing properly fitting clothes	Wearing clean clothes
	Following verbal directions
Identifying symptoms of illness	Basic first aid
	Communication with others
Carrying identification card	Using the telephone
Dressing for weather conditions	Feeding oneself
	Shopping for needed items
Sexual awareness	Managing money
Using appliances	Planning for the future
General repairs	Maintaining a household
Preparing meals	

Many of these goals are subgoals that fall under another of these headings. And each subgoal can be further broken into steps needed to accomplish the goal. Group members can arrange these steps in the sequence that one actually would go through to accomplish the activity.

COMMUNITY AWARENESS

Community awareness skills represent one of the final steps toward eventual independence. They are developed after the person is functioning independently. Community awareness skills focus on improving an understanding of the community in which the individual lives, teaching the skills necessary for access to community resources and for moving safely through the community. The world can be a very frightening place but familiarity gives the individual greater freedom to move through it and the survival skills necessary to avoid being exploited.

The continuum of skills may range from learning to read signs (stop, go, walk, danger) to providing access to medical appointments, shopping, police, and fire department telephone numbers. Again, these skills are important to learn before moving to an independent living situation.

With practice and supervision, these skills can be developed and learned. It may be a good idea to use the community as a laboratory and demonstrate exactly how to do certain things (e.g., use a laudromat, make a call from a pay phone, order food from a menu, reach a destination by bus).

To prepare groups for this phase of skill development, identify all available community resources, with each group member picking a topic or agency to investigate. Compile this information into a community resource handbook. The book can list those agencies that service basic needs at no charge or at a minimal cost. Be short, specific, and simplify the processes for obtaining such things as food stamps and general assistance. Include maps, phone numbers, and addresses; do not include generalizations that only staff members would understand. The topics may include the following:

How to call Information

How to use a pay telephone

How to call and report a fire

How to call the police for assistance

How to make a medical appointment

How to obtain free clothing

How to use day work programs

How to find lodging in rooming houses

How to get free food

How to use crisis services

How to use volunteer services

How to use employment services

How to use transportation services

How to use dial-a-ride programs

How to get food stamps

How to apply for Social Security benefits

How to use winterizing programs

How to get free meals and shelter

How to find apartments for rent

How to get fuel assistance

How to get general assistance

How to use day care

How to use banks

How to use emergency shelters

Hundreds of topics can be included that are specific to each group. Getting specific is the key. Find out what each agency does, or do not include it. The best process for determining what is needed is to examine the problems that confront group members daily in taking care of their needs. It often has proved helpful to record the process by which a particular problem has been solved, such as obtaining Social Security. After determining what forms are required, who must be contacted, and the steps to be gone through, write down the entire process for future reference. The emotionally disturbed individual, in fact, will have to go through a similar process to solve his or her own problems. The following list of community resources can be visited on a group outing, which will improve community awareness.

Post office
Train station or airport
Taxi stands
Gardening shops
Department stores
Resale shops
Hobby shops
Drug stores
Furniture stores
Fire and police departments
Bike shops
Key shops
Civic centers
Restaurants
Museums
Movie theaters
Grocery stores or supermarkets
Bus station
Hardware stores
Car dealers
Schools
Laundromats
Bookstores
Car washes
Hospitals and clinics
Banks
Social services
Churches
Libraries
Plumbers
Parks
Room and board homes

VOCATIONAL SKILLS

Finding a job is difficult for anyone. It requires preparation, experience, and education, as well as an opportunity to prove oneself. Even with all these advantages, it is still difficult to find a job and earn a living. This is a hundred times more difficult for the emotionally disturbed. These individuals probably lack many opportunities for education and experience. They have the same wants and desires as others: to own a car, a house; have a family, a meaningful relationship with another person; live on their own; and to have control over their own destiny.

To begin preparing for a vocation requires a thorough assessment of interests and skill levels. Begin the process of assessment by noting down all the employment experiences or skills of the person. This will provide a foundation on which to begin building vocational skills. Consider these questions in the assessment process: How much schooling does the person currently have? If no high school diploma, can the person qualify for a General Educational Diploma (GED)? Is this person qualified for vocational training? Does the person have the necessary work habits required to hold a job?

An occupational therapy group can be established at your program to develop work-oriented skills. You can establish a work activity program or sheltered workshop where you actually manufacture a product to sell. There are a number of ideas for products to make or assemble that can be broken down into easy steps and assigned to different people.

One center produces wooden cratelike planters. Individuals at the center cut them to size, sand, and stain them; others assemble and package them for sale. Other centers make scratch pads. People at the center cut donated paper to size, place it into a form, and paint glue on one side. It is sold to local office supply companies or other businesses. Other ideas can be obtained from your local library through the *Thomas Manufacturing* manuals, published annually. This catalogue has a picture of every product made in the United States. In addition, it has the names and addresses of the companies that make them. You may want to write a company to investigate whether you can contract with them to assemble different parts of a product. Each project helps develop the necessary work habits an individual must have to compete in the job market. Seeing something they have made also increases the motivation and self-esteem of those who worked on it, which is extremely important if they are to be successful in the working environment. Other job-related group activities to focus on might include:

Identifying skills
Following up on employment possibilities
Accepting supervision
Identifying proper work breaks
Following rules
Seeking and performing odd jobs
Coming to work on time
Doing volunteer work
Cooperating with others
Accepting criticism
Completing tasks
Seeking help when needed
Filling out job applications
Preparing a resume
Identifying and correcting mistakes
Developing maintenance skills
Seeking and performing day work
Working with ceramics
Working on wood projects
Creating block prints
Performing tool work, assembly work
Working on leather crafts
Painting

Filling out job application forms is time-consuming, frustrating, and requires practice. Group members can be helped to prepare a resume, fill out job forms, and practice job interviews. The resume should cover all the important information, such as experience, references, and the reason the person is unemployed. Rehearsing the interview will help increase self-confidence. The questions to be asked should be those most likely to be asked during the interview session. The feedback should concentrate on answers, appearance, posture, and skill level. Rehearsing these techniques may take some of the fear out of applying for a job. A videotape camera, if available, can be used to show group members how they appear to others. A less expensive idea is to use a simple tape recorder so they can listen to their own voices after the interviewing process.

EDUCATION

The best way to prepare for independence is through the educational process. Determining what kind of work group members would like to pursue should indicate what type of schooling they will need. A number of free or low-cost programs are available to help this population. Become familiar with the financial aid and grant process at local educational institutions—how to apply, and who is qualified. Such knowledge of the resources in the area can be an invaluable skill for assisting these people. Another consideration is that some programs require psychological testing prior to admission to a training program. If so, make arrangements in advance of the referral for testing in order to obtain quick turnaround time on the results. Have a specific reason for requesting testing evaluations. This will help determine what tests and information are needed. Be realistic with the individual about the job market and what will be required of him or her to be successful. There is nothing more frustrating than to complete a program and not be able to find a job. Some skill development areas that can be worked on in a group include:

Reading	Writing
Mathematics	Budgeting
Vocational training	Specialty classes
Typing	Goal setting
Telling time	Identifying measures
Check writing	Communication of ideas
Developing outside interests	Socialization
	History
Current events	Government
Voting	Cooking
Spelling	Nutrition
Comparison shopping	Bookkeeping
Science	

LEISURE TIME ACTIVITIES

One of the times most difficult for emotionally disturbed individuals is when they have nothing to do. For them, as for anyone else, leisure-time activities need to be developed.

If it is true that "the best things in life are free," this is the chance to prove it. Usually, practitioners will be working with scarce resources, and their clients, too, will have to manage within tight budgets. This means practitioners have to be resourceful and creative with what is available. For example, places often give away things, such as scraps of wood, paper, etc., if someone will ask whether they can haul away the unwanted items. This provides a supply of materials to work with on a creative project. Another idea is to go to garage sales, where usable items sell at a fraction of the original cost. Some other leisure-time activities that can be explored in groups include:

Going to the movies
Shopping
Taking walks
Collecting
Playing cards and games
Watching television
Reading newspapers
Exercising
Gardening
Having parties
Photography
Drawing
Crafts
Weaving
Playing an instrument
Keeping a journal
Visiting the zoo

Attending sporting activities
Working on hobbies
Building things
Going out to eat
Listening to stereo or radio
Sewing
Taking care of pets
Community recreation
Taking trips
Writing stories
Dancing
Swimming
Fishing
Cooking
Singing

ART THERAPY GROUPS

Art is used as a symbolic therapeutic means of eliciting emotional information and expression. By its very nature art is projective, coming from deep within the individual, and usually requires interpretation. Art therapists have years of training in projective interpretation and are skilled at deciphering the symbolic material presented by the individual. Art helps facilitate unconscious feelings and thoughts regarding any conflicts, values, and perceptions of the world. Art work may produce a flood of unconscious emotional material. Therefore, care must

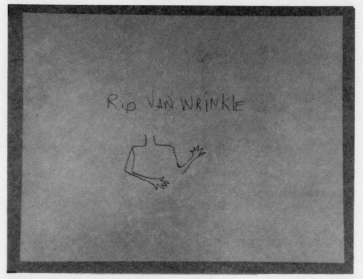

*Figure 7.1. "Rip Van Wrinkle," a family
portrait.*

be taken when considering a projective assignment. Without
comprehensive background information on an individual, the
assignment may affect the individual in unexpected ways.

For example, simply asking an individual to draw his or her
family may sound innocent enough, but if a family member has
died, this drawing activity may trigger the individual to decompensate. Figure 7.1 indicates this situation. The father of the
person who drew this picture had just died. Although he was
requested to draw the entire family, and he had numerous sib-
lings, none appeared. His actual title is "Rip Van Wrinkle,"
which may reflect something that is old and dying. There is some
ambivalence toward the father with the reference to Rip Van
Winkle, who went to sleep and left forever. His portrayal of his
father as decapitated may indicate very strong feelings of hatred
that could not be expressed any way other than in the drawing.

Another example of a family drawing is shown in Figure
7.2. The individual draws himself among the other children in
the family, but his mother's image is enlarged and dominates
the picture. The cold, domineering, and perhaps overbearing

Figure 7.2. Family portrait.

mother leaves little doubt who runs the family. His father's image is the second largest in the composition. It seems to be an image of passivity, ineffectiveness, as if he is missing or gone most of the time. The children, mice-like in proportion to the other figures, are withdrawn to the corner of the page, isolated, alone, and scared. This haunting picture leaves little doubt about who the significant members of this family are.

If it is true that a picture is worth a thousand words, then you will have a considerable amount of information available to you about a person. Art can be used to help clarify difficult issues that cannot be expressed verbally; it can be an endless source of insight and skill development. The art produced by an emotionally disturbed individual must be spontaneous and expressive, viewed nonjudgmentally, and have value in establishing a trusting relationship with the person. Participating in a group and sharing drawings with others may be a goal in the area of interpersonal communication. Art is an important activity to include in group work and will prove to be both fun and therapeutic at the same time. Some suggested topics for art therapy are:

Draw a self-portrait

Draw a person

Draw your family

Draw anything you want

Draw something emotional

Draw cartoons

Draw a memory

Draw what will happen a
  year from now

Draw an animal you would
  like to be

Draw what you like best

Draw a story

Draw a sad place

Draw a happy place

Draw your neighborhood

Draw a moment you would
  like to relive

Draw a house

Draw a famous person

Draw a famous event

Draw a tree

Draw masks

Draw a fantasy

Draw a person in the rain

Draw your room

Scribble

Draw your own story

Draw treasured objects

Draw your community

Draw a dream

Draw your family tree

Draw an expectation

Draw a hero

Draw a season

Draw a lonely place

Draw a relaxing place

Draw a holiday

Draw love

Draw old people

Draw children

Draw an activity

Fill a circle

Getting the group members to a point of independence is an uphill battle, with numerous setbacks and revisions of treatment plans. This brings us to the most important element in assuring the successful treatment of this group of people; that is, taking care of oneself.

Maintaining one's own energy level when running your group is essential. It is extremely demanding to be "on" all the time. In addition, group leaders are subject to emotional drains almost continuously from group members, who are attempting to fill their own emotional void. The leaders must be able to replenish themselves emotionally, intellectually, spiritually, and physically. Practitioners cannot help others if they are burned out or too tired to move. Therefore, it is imperative to decrease the stress level as much as possible, to be organized, to plan ahead, to set goals and know how to reach them. When group leaders work, they should work hard; but their play should be embraced with the same passion. Having outside interests and activities will make life interesting and fulfilling. Being excited about life, learning all the time, trying to be the best one can be—all this creates a positive attitude and an energy level that is contagious to others. By being friendly, honest, and open, one will find that one's goals are easier to achieve.

Successful groups seem to take on a life of their own and seem to be greater than the sum of their members. Groups provide a means for effective interpersonal communication and interaction among people. As a whole, groups are more effective problem solvers than any one individual. Group members have feelings of belonging and emerge with unconditional acceptance. The group becomes self-maintaining, conscious of both the task and each member's individual needs. The overall trust level of the group increases to the point that group members know each other better than anyone else. Because the group is safe, members readily can try on new and different behaviors in the attempt to find themselves. Members learn to give and receive feedback among one another in a positive and constructive manner. Because this was the main purpose for beginning the group, the group now is ready to say good-bye to each other.

This is a very difficult process as the members return to their separate lives, but perhaps they have gained the confidence to enter into new relationships more readily. They have learned to accept others for who they are and have developed an understanding of the common bond with all humanity. Perhaps, in the pain of separation, the members are transformed into new individuals with improved skills and new aspirations for the future.

8. Friday 4:45 P.M.
Crisis Intervention

The chief goal of crisis intervention is to reestablish the functioning level of the individual to the point that existed prior to the crisis. Many crises appear to happen suddenly, but this image actually may reflect a period of sustained coping by the individual that has suddenly broken down, resulting in the appearance of a crisis. Following this line of thought, one can assume that the individual must have been functioning at least minimally prior to the crisis. The goal then becomes reestablishing this equilibrium of normality in the individual's life.

All people are subjected to crises at some time in their lives, but with experience, they have learned to cope with them. The crises that a person experiences may vary in frequency and intensity, such as the loss of a family member, a midlife crisis, or the ultimate life-threatening crisis of suicide. Although, by their nature, crises vary from individual to individual, one factor remains constant: a breakdown in the individual's ability to cope or adjust to a new situation.

Practitioners must have the skills to resolve a crisis effectively. They can begin by focusing on resolving the individual's immediate problem, which has precipitated the presenting crisis. Obviously, having a good idea of the circumstances involved in a crisis will increase the ability to intervene quickly and effectively. Slaikeu (1984, p. 123) has listed five areas that are important to consider when attempting to resolve a crisis situation. The responses to these following questions will be of assistance in obtaining a clear picture of the crisis situation.

146

1. What are the precipitating events, those that led to this crisis?
2. Specifically what is the presenting problem?
3. What is the environmental context of the problem?
4. How was the individual functioning before the crisis?
5. How is the individual functioning now?

WHAT HAPPENED?

The first questions that come to mind when evaluating any crisis situation are What happened? and What events led to this crisis? In other words, What are the precipitating events that triggered this immediate crisis? In most cases, something has happened that, figuratively speaking, has been the last snowflake that broke the tree branch. The individual in crisis feels overwhelmed by circumstances and is no longer able to cope with any additional stress. One should realize that even though this most recent situation was the cause of the current feelings of being overwhelmed, this is probably not the only stressor in the person's life. This is especially true with the emotionally disturbed individual, whose inability to solve one problem results in an accumulation of problems. As this enormous mountain of problems grows, so do the feelings of being overwhelmed. The individual no longer has the ability to cope with the stress and adjust to life's pressures. He or she is flooded with overwhelming feelings of confusion, helplessness, and perhaps even hopelessness.

THE PRESENTING PROBLEM

The next step to evaluate is What is the presenting problem? Pursuing this issue is the starting point for resolving the present crisis. Concentrating all efforts on the resolution of the immediate concern may be the only way of restoring the individual's prior functioning level.

By clearly defining the problem, one then can focus on resolving it. The resolution of the presenting problem seems to be twofold in nature. First, the ability to solve the individual's

immediate concern is enhanced by using all of the skills and resources available. Second, sometimes the precipitating problem cannot be actually resolved, such as a death of a loved one, but providing the necessary emotional support may be enough to give the person the strength to cope with the situation again. One should not underestimate the value of our personal, nonjudgmental support and warmth. Sometimes, all that is needed is for someone to listen to the individual's concerns. This alone may help the person unravel the mixture of his or her confusing thoughts and feelings.

ENVIRONMENTAL INFLUENCES

The third question to ask when intervening in a crisis situation is How does the environment interplay with the individual in crisis? Most crises do not happen in a vacuum. The environment in which one lives is intricately interwoven into one's life. The individual lives in an environment that can provide support or emphasize alienation and loneliness.

Determining and activating a network of support will lead to quicker resolution of the crisis. This is especially true if the person is continuing to live in or returning to the same environment where the crisis originally developed. Assisting the individual to find patterns of support through friends, family, and significant others is one of the goals of crisis intervention.

Folk systems of support for the individual in crisis is a concept that is beginning to come to the forefront among crisis intervention workers. A question arises: How were individuals in crisis taken care of prior to community mental health systems or crisis intervention programs? In answering this question, it becomes apparent that folk systems existed in all communities. They are the individual's personal support systems such as physicians, police, ministers, concerned friends, family, and neighbors. Perhaps, considering where referrals come from will provide an important clue to the folk systems existing within the community.

When reacting to a crisis, consideration of the whole individual is necessary, including the environment in which he or she works and lives. These are essential components of a successful crisis intervention strategy.

PRIOR FUNCTIONING

The fourth question that must be asked is How was the individual functioning prior to the crisis? Was the person functioning adequately prior to the crisis—working, going to school, and maintaining a household? If he or she was, this may indicate that the support the individual needs already is available within his or her life. Without such support, this may be just another crisis in a long line of crises that have been emerging as a pattern for some time.

Unfortunately, the severely emotionally disturbed often fall into this latter pattern of crisis. Intervention with certain individuals takes place only when a crisis is present. The person seems to seek help only during these crisis periods; however, such crisis intervention never achieves a permanent solution: the fires it puts out always seem to reappear elsewhere. More intense and in-depth follow-up treatment is needed. At times, follow-up care will be resisted, primarily because people find it difficult to admit that something is wrong. Denial of problems frequently leads one to blame external forces for the creation of the problems. Accepting the need for long-term treatment is difficult and may be perceived by the individual as an admission of guilt for the present situation. Follow-up care should instill the necessary coping patterns and problem-solving skills to achieve a long-term solution.

It is difficult to accept responsibility for one's life and all the problems within it. But it is essential that this fact be accepted before true resolution of problems can begin to take place.

CURRENT FUNCTIONING

The last question asked in the evaluation of a crisis is How is the individual functioning now? Is the individual safe? Answering these questions will guide the immediate actions to be taken. The assessment of a dangerous situation should be determined immediately. Is the person coping with the crisis? How lethal is the situation? These two factors determine the extent to which intervention by an outsider can take place. Is the individual at a life-threatening point? Most of the time when an individual contacts crisis intervention workers, the situation has escalated to a point where some immediate intervention must take place. At these times, the option of referring such an individual to another professional is not always a luxury available. Practitioners must be prepared to act in the most effective way necessary to preserve the life of the individual; everything else is secondary.

Forecasting the future is a skill everyone would like to have. Fortunately, it is possible to develop the ability to predict the potential for a crisis by becoming aware of certain cues that may indicate the need to intervene in a situation before it becomes critical. The effectiveness of assisting an individual through a crisis requires intervention as quickly as possible.

Halpern attempted to define crisis empirically, by comparing the behavior of people not experiencing crisis to the behavior of people undergoing crisis. Persons in crisis experienced the following constellation of symptoms significantly more than those not in crisis (Halpern, 1973, pp. 342–349):

1. Feelings of tiredness and exhaustion
2. Feelings of helplessness
3. Feelings of inadequacy
4. Feelings of confusion
5. Physical symptoms
6. Feelings of anxiety
7. Disorganization of functioning in work relationships
8. Disorganization of functioning in family relationships
9. Disorganization of functioning in social relationships
10. Disorganization in social activities

In summary, the chief goal in crisis intervention is to help the individual regain control of his or her life, with a primary focus on restoring the individual's coping and problem-solving ability to at least the level of functioning prior to the crisis.

It was Friday at 4:45 P.M., when most crises seem to happen. The woman on the phone indicated that she was a manager of a local hotel. She was calling about a man who currently lived in the hotel. When cleaning his room, the maid had found little white tablets scattered on the floor, and during the day, the man seemed confused and disoriented. When asked for a more specific description, she said that she had seen him riding the elevator up and down throughout the previous night, having difficulty deciding whether to get off. When she offered assistance, he just mumbled to himself and closed the elevator door. She was concerned about the man's general welfare: whether he was eating properly and sleeping. And because of the quantity of pills found in his room, she also was concerned about the possibility of an accidental suicide. The policy of the community mental health center was to go to a person's home in an emergency. My center was familiar with this man and thought it would be appropriate to see him directly. I assured her that I would be right there to speak with him to evaluate the situation.

The man in question had been involved in various programs in the past, so I was somewhat familiar with the case. I had requested the chart from our secretary in order to assess the background information on this individual; in particular, the diagnosis and the medication he was prescribed. Both of these factors helped in determining the extent of immediate risk to the individual. He was diagnosed schizophrenic and was currently on an antipsychotic medication, mellaril. I immediately checked the *Physicians' Desk Reference* (PDR) photographic section, to verify whether the medication in question was that found by the maid. In a potential suicidal crisis, it is important to note the first paragraph of the PDR listing, where it indicates the type of drug and how it is used therapeutically. Then, I referred to the section on overdose manifestations, which gave me a brief description of some of the various symptoms that might indicate an overdose. Being familiar with this information gave me a cue of what symptoms to look for, which in fact might save the man's life in an emergency.

A secretary can be an important resource in a crisis. In this particular case, the secretary was able to check who was presently working with the individual and made arrangements for a familiar person to meet us down at the hotel. Having a trusting relationship already established with the individual in a crisis is an invaluable resource. In addition, the secretary was able to check on the availability of emergency resources: poison control information, psychiatric hospital vacancies, and respite care settings available for emergency placements. All this information could be obtained by phone and relayed to the worker on the scene.

Arriving at the hotel, we had the person at the desk request that the individual come down to the lobby. Since we were still evaluating the seriousness of the situation, we had to be considered only as visitors. Everyone has the right to privacy. Therefore, the evaluation, based upon a second-hand report, required the least intrusive assessment possible.

The individual appeared somewhat disheveled, in an old T-shirt and torn jeans, even though it was winter and cold in the lobby. It appeared evident from his mannerisms that he was depressed, his speech pressured, and that he had not slept during the night. When asked whether he had eaten recently, he claimed he had not eaten for a few days because he had no money. At this time, he seemed oriented to time, place, and person; that is, he knew where he was and who we were. There was no evidence of delusions or active hallucinations. Although he did not appear to be overtly dangerous to himself, it was obvious that he was not taking good care of himself. We questioned him regarding any depression and suicidal thoughts he may have been having. He indicated that he felt lonely and depressed. Then we inquired about the white tablets found in his room. He stated they were vitamin C. We also inquired whether he was taking the medication that was prescribed for him, and he replied that he had thrown out this medication because it did not help him. It did not appear from our interview that he would be harmful to others or was suicidal at this point in time. If we allowed him to go on untreated, however, he certainly would come to harm at some point.

When evaluating the emotionally disturbed individual in crisis, three factors are examined. First, does the person pose a danger to him- or herself or others? Second, is the individual able to care for his or her basic needs? Third, does the person understand the need for treatment? In this particular situation the second criterion was met; he was unable to care for his basic needs because he was not eating properly or dressing appropriately for the weather conditions. When asked about taking his medication, he stated he did not need it because he was not crazy, everyone else was crazy. These statements are fairly common with the emotionally disturbed. Perhaps this indicated that he did not understand his need for treatment.

Usually, an individual who does not meet the first criterion of danger to him- or herself or others will not require 24-hour inpatient supervision and probably will not require commitment into a psychiatric facility. The next alternative for placement should be in the least restrictive setting where the individual can be maintained safely. In this case, temporary placement in a group home, respite care, or adult foster care facility would be indicated, with intense follow-up treatment.

The initial contact with a person is extremely important. By providing the safety net into which an individual can fall, the network of mental health services becomes responsible for the individual's treatment and care.

It was obvious, at this point, that the individual could not care for his basic needs. A respite care placement in a group home was indicated until the individual felt he could go out on his own again. Respite care is a temporary stay where the individual's basic needs for food, clothing, and shelter can be addressed. This type of treatment was pursued, and the individual was grateful for our assistance.

INABILITY TO CARE FOR BASIC NEEDS

Inability to take care of one's basic needs, such as food, clothing, and shelter, can result in a crisis. Fortunately, society has a safety net to discover and assist most of the homeless and helpless individuals before they meet with an untimely end. These are crises of neglect, in contrast to conscious attempts to end their own existence. In order to intervene effectively in crises of neglect, practitioners must be aware of the resources in the community. They also must be aware of the entire process for obtaining assistance. Most general assistance programs, unfortunately, are complicated and time-consuming to apply for. The process may seem exaggerated even further at times of crisis. But, in the end, the long-term benefits of obtaining professional assistance are well worthwhile and far outweigh any immediate delays.

Knowing what resources are available and being prepared can speed up the overall process and avoid delays. Most agencies have specific criteria and eligibility requirements for those they serve. Therefore, being familiar with both provides a better idea of what resources are viable in a particular situation.

To some extent, almost every nonprofit corporation in the community services individuals' basic needs; these nonprofit corporations would include mental health and social services, religious organizations, and community service clubs. It may be a good idea to organize an interagency committee of all the service agencies in the area to share information and establish a referral network. But even without such a formal organization, having a personal contact person in each different agency is an invaluable resource. These people can share information about what specifically is required for assistance and provide help in assessing difficult cases. The primary concern should be with helping the individual in crisis. Locating resources in your community is a difficult task; yet it would be even more difficult for the person in crisis to gain access to these resources if the expertise of a practitioner were not available.

INABILITY TO UNDERSTAND THE NEED
FOR TREATMENT

When people have physical problems, they seldom deny that they are hurt, bleeding, or have a broken limb. The emotionally disturbed, however, commonly deny that they need help at all. Whether this is a symptom of the disorder or a defense mechanism to preserve personal dignity, the emotionally disturbed individual finds it difficult to admit to having problems. This denial also is difficult for families and friends to accept when working with the individual. Probably they have attempted to intercede with the person numerous times to prevent a crisis from developing or escalating. They have attempted to talk to the person about his or her thoughts or behavior as though the individual was rational and purposely behaving that way. The emotionally disturbed individual feels disoriented, delusional, frightened, and confused, perhaps more frightened than anyone else about his or her feelings, thoughts, and behavior. Nevertheless, sometimes the individual does not believe that he or she is different from anyone else. Some believe that the voices they hear are actually spirits from different worlds. Some actually believe that they are unique and special because of the voices they hear. In these cases, the denial may reflect that the person does not understand the need for treatment.

Individuals in crisis have been struggling with their emotional disorders and probably are frightened by their lack of personal control over their thoughts, feelings, and emotions. Practitioners intervene with treatment plans by providing the individuals with external control of the situation, where they lack the internal control. The goal then becomes the reestablishment of a sense of internal control within the person. The individuals should have as much control over the treatment plan as possible, but only to the point to which they feel comfortable handling it. In the future, individual control and responsibility can be increased gradually.

One should be aware that increases in responsibility come with a direct and proportional increase in stress. This can produce overwhelming anxiety for the troubled person and lead to their greatest fear: the lack of internal control, the feeling of being swallowed up by the disorder. In clinical settings, researchers have found that individuals do better with external limits and structure during a crisis period. By having structure, they are able to make their world predictable, thus lowering their feels of anxiety.

Acceptance by individuals that there may be something wrong with them is never easy and, even under the best of situations, denial plays a role in final acceptance. Numerous myths about mental illness stand in the way of such acceptance, both for individuals and their families. The individuals and their families carry a considerable burden of guilt and distorted thinking regarding emotional disturbance. "Have I been a bad parent? Could I have done something different to prevent this 'mental illness'?" The sooner these issues are handled in treatment the better, thereby clearing the way for acceptance and treatment of the disorder. A clear understanding of the problem, as well as insight into the cause and treatment alternatives, will help both the individuals and their families.

DEPRESSION

Crises typically do not happen without a component of depression. Whether an individual is suicidal or simply unable to care for his or her basic needs, depression always seems to be present. Depression is the most common and frequently reported of all psychiatric disorders (Kline, 1974). Fortunately, it also has the best prognosis for recovery. When assessing an individual for depression, the three most common symptoms are a depressed mood, the loss of interest in daily activities, and anxiety, closely followed by symptoms of insomnia, loss of appetite, lack of energy, and fatigability, together with the beginnings of suicidal thoughts (Paykel, 1982). Depression can build up over a period of time, beginning with symptoms so mild that the individual does not really know when it actually began. Emotionally disturbed individuals are at the greatest risk of potential suicide if they have suffered a prolonged depression and see no hope for the future.

There are many causes of depression, from endocrine imbalances to failure to live up to one's expectations in life. In some instances, depression results from the inability to integrate the reality of life with one's own expectations of oneself. No matter what life has in store, people have control over how they choose to react to it. People's expectations are products of their perceptions, interests, and personally held beliefs, values, and attitudes. These aspects of the individual must be examined in order to treat depression effectively. Treating the causes of depression offers the best possibility of generating a long-term solution to this type of crisis.

Everyone has experienced depression at one time or another, but in the emotionally disturbed, the severity is measured by its intensity and duration. No doubt, during this time of crisis, the individual has been sending out signals to friends and family but has been unsuccessful in obtaining the needed help because of his or her overwhelming feelings of confusion and mixture of emotions. The depressed individual reaches a point where he or she no longer can cope with the intensity of the feelings, nor can he or she easily interpret and communicate their thoughts and feelings to others. Many times, the thoughts of the individual, by their nature, are distorted; but the individual reacts to them as if they were real, struggling to maintain some type of personal control over an uncontrollable environment. Examining the thinking process of chronically depressed individuals will point out certain mental images that such people unconsciously may use to maintain this level of depression. This mental image usually is a product of some type of distorted thinking. Table 8.1 lists some common types of distorted thinking.

SUICIDE

Suicide may be best understood as an aggressive retaliatory act toward significant figures in the individual's present life or toward fantasies of significant figures in his past. The primary motivating fantasy includes the wish to hurt someone else, with the belief that suicide will accomplish this end. The individual imagines how sorry or guilty people will feel if he dies. (Karon & Vandenbos, 1981, p. 262)

The individual who attempts suicide obviously is in crisis, although this current crisis is not necessarily the sole reason for the suicide attempt. Actual suicides are not spontaneous actions but have been thought about for some time, during which the person has been ambivalent. *Ambivalence* is the simultaneous attraction toward and repulsion by some type of action or decision, or the simultaneous attraction toward mutually exclusive actions or decisions. The ambivalence about wanting to live or die has been resolved by the actual decision to commit suicide. The individual has come to believe that this course of action is the only alternative available.

Table 8.1
COMMON MISCONCEPTIONS ABOUT THE SELF, WORLD, GOALS, AND IDEALS

1. Distorted Self-Definitions
   a. I am a helpless, innocent victim. Unhappiness and what occurs in life is caused by outside circumstances or past events for which I am not responsible and have no control.
   b. I am not attractive, feminine, or manly enough.
   c. I am deficient (e.g., not smart enough), and therefore destined to fail.
   d. I am wicked.
   e. I am weak (and need to be led).
   f. I am so exceptional that I am entitled to my own way (narcissistic entitlement).
   g. I am undesirable and no one could love me.
   h. My worth is measured by my performance.
   i. I am worthless if my spouse (girlfriend, boyfriend, mother, father, child) does not love me.

2. Mistaken Assumptions About People and the World
   a. Life is a dangerous, dog-eat-dog, jungle. (People are hostile competitors.)
   b. Life doesn't give me a chance, and I'm destined to fail.
   c. Men (women) cannot be trusted.
   d. Life is chaotic and completely unpredictable.
   e. People are stupid, and one ought to take them for all he/she can.
   f. Other people are happy, "normal," and do not have feelings or problems similar to mine. In fact, some people have perfect marriages, perfect children, and so forth.
   g. Good looks, superior intelligence, athletic ability, money, and so forth, make one happy.
   h. People will look down on me as inept if I make or admit mistakes, admit limitations, and seek advice.
   i. Most things are either black or white, that is, good-bad, right-wrong, liked or disliked, clever or stupid, attractive or unattractive.

3. Mistaken, Self-Defeating Goals
   a. It is essential to be perfect, completely competent, and without flaw to be worthwhile. Don't make or admit mistakes.
   b. I must be loved and approved of (admired, liked) by everyone; I must never offend.
   c. I must find the perfect or "right" solution.

    d. I have to be the best, the first, or right.

    e. I must be the center of attention, the star attraction.

    f. I must be dependent on someone stronger to protect and lead me.

    g. I should retaliate and get even with the world.

    h. I must not let people know what I am really like (they may think less of me or use what they learn against me).

    i. I must ventilate anger whenever I feel it.

    j. I must be safe and secure at all times. I must be careful not to take any risks or chances.

    k. I must be completely self-sufficient and independent.

4. Mistaken Ideals

    a. The only thing worth being is a "star" (or genius). Nothing less is worth working for.

    b. I should always be calm, cool, and collected and never lose control.

    c. I should always know the right answer.

    d. I should be the perfect spouse, parent, lover, employee, son, daughter, church member.

    e. A "real" man is a tough guy who never takes any guff from anyone.

    f. A "real" woman should always be feminine, nonoffensive, unassertive, and dependent.

    g. I should always have my own way.

    h. I have an easier/happier life when I avoid responsibilities and problems.

    i. I should be able to succeed and be happy without discomfort or struggle.

    j. I should always be unselfish, considerate, generous, happy.

    k. The purpose of life is to work hard and to be productive—not happy.

    l. If you try hard enough you can excel at anything and everything.

Source: From *"Multidimensional psychotherapy: A counselors' guide for the map form"* by D. C. Hammond and K. Stanfield. Copyright 1977 by the Institute for Personality and Ability Testing, Inc. Reprinted by permission.

Anyone who has worked with crises is aware that there are apparent patterns to the crises at any particular time; this also is true with suicides. In Durkheim's classical studies of seasonal suicides, he confirmed the social factors that influence suicidal patterns. His findings suggested that the six warmest months showed the highest instances of suicidal acts in Europe. He also found that the majority of suicides happened more frequently during the day than at night. Durkheim theorized that when social life increased in intensity, suicide was more likely to occur. These are interesting findings for those who intervene in crises, and they provide additional cues for evaluating the potential suicidal individual.

At 3:45 A.M., a woman called. Her voice was slow and quiet and she was crying as she began telling me of her loneliness. She claimed to be very depressed and had been drinking all night. She stated that a half hour ago, she had taken an entire bottle of pills but she changed her mind and did not want to die. She cried, "Please help me!"

Reassuring her that everything would be okay, I began asking questions: Where do you live? What is the address? What did you take? How much did you have to drink? How long ago? What is your phone number? What is your name, if you want to give it? After she answered a few questions, the phone dropped to the floor and there was no answer on the other end of the line. Having assessed that this was a critical situation, I immediately called an ambulance, which was sent to her home. If two telephone lines are available, the crisis worker always should maintain contact with the individual to keep him or her talking and conscious, while using the other line to obtain help. If only one line is available, as in this case, the worker should hang up and begin phoning for help.

Next, an immediate call was made to the local police in order to inform them of the emergency and request assistance. They acted quickly and were able to meet the ambulance at the scene. This was necessary in order to gain entrance inside the house, since the caller was unconscious at this point.

The procedures of the Hot Line required calling the hospital and making the emergency room aware of a possible admission. Giving the hospital all the possible information available on the crisis prepared them better for their intervention. Obviously, time is a critical factor in any life-threatening situation, so having everyone prepared for the crisis is the best course of action.

The next step was to call the police again, in order to let them know which hospital was available to receive her. Then a call was placed to the nearest poison control center to find out how toxic the drugs were when taken in combination with alcohol and whether there was an antidote. Another call to the hospital shared this information, along with the phone number of the poison control center contacted.

After informing the hospital of the recommendations from the poison control center, the decision was made to meet the woman at the hospital. At this particular point, I had done all I could do to save the individual's life. But by being on the scene, I was available to answer some of the questions the hospital staff had regarding the situation.

The crisis was over for now and the woman's life was saved. By working as a team, the crisis worker, physicians, nurses, police, and ambulance attendants had done together what no one could do alone. The next day, a follow-up referral was made for outpatient counseling. Even during her stay in the hospital, the woman was seen daily for counseling and scheduled for continued outpatient assistance upon discharge.

Assessment

When assessing a potential suicide, two prominent factors need to be kept in mind: (1) What seems to be the plan for committing suicide? If there is a plan and a method, the person has given some thought to the matter prior to contacting you. For example, has the individual borrowed a gun recently or hoarded some type of medication? (2) Next, if you have been seeing the individual for some time, was there a marked change in attitude? With the potentially suicidal individual, usually, after a prolonged depression, the person suddenly seems happy and at peace. On the surface, this may appear very good, indicating to you that he or she is getting better. In some cases this may be true, especially if something has changed for the better with the person's life. But, in other cases, this may signal that the person has made a decision to die and now is free of the burden of indecision.

George Atwood (1972, pp. 284–285) offers three criteria that may help differentiate between the individual who is actually getting better and the one at high risk of suicide:

1. The individual who is improving will have increased insight into his or her depression, whereas the individual at risk will show no increase in insight.
2. The individual who is improving will talk more about the future as he or she improves, whereas the person about to commit suicide will not discuss the future.
3. The individual who is improving will become more willing to discuss suicide, whereas the individual who has decided to commit suicide will not be willing to discuss it.

If all three of these criteria align closely in the same direction, the risk of eventual suicide should be clear.

When involved with assessing the potential for suicide or during the actual crisis, the answer to a number of these questions will prove helpful:

1. Is the attempt currently in progress, and where, physically, is the individual?
2. Are drugs and/or alcohol involved? Alcohol decreases impulse control and a stimulant may give the depressed individual enough energy to attempt suicide.
3. Have any notes been left or final arrangements made? Are any weapons accessible?
4. Is the individual giving away possessions? This is a clear signal because one does not need possessions if one does not have a future.
5. Have there been other attempts? There sometimes are many attempts at suicide to get help or attention from others. One can become desensitized to an individual who always claims to be committing suicide for attention. The danger is that the person one day will be successful, whether by accident or design. All suicide attempts must be treated as real. With these individuals, treatment must begin by showing them how to get attention by other means. In a number of cases, these individuals need external control since they feel so out of control of their own lives. Attempt to structure their lives until they are able to regain control for themselves.
6. Does the person have other support systems or is he or she alone? Can family or friends stay with the person through the crisis? A person who is alone is at greater risk of committing suicide.

7. What has changed in the person's life recently that motivated this step? Did the person lose a loved one or a job?
Do any major health problems make suicide seem to be the
best decision?

Table 8.2 describes ten factors associated with attempts at
suicide. Following are four groups of characteristics (syn-
dromes) that Farberow, Helif, and Litman (1970) consider
clues for identifying potential suicides.

The Depressed. The individual seems withdrawn, apathetic,
apprehensive, and anxious; often "blue" and tearful; somewhat
unreachable and seemingly uncaring. The person increasingly
is unwilling to communicate; talking seems harder; there are
fewer spontaneous remarks; answers are shorter or even mono-
syllabic. Facial expressions are less lively, the posture is more
drooped, gestures are less animated, the gait is less springy,
and the individual's mind seems occupied elsewhere. Often the
individual reflects attitudes such as "I don't care," "What does
it matter," or "It's no use anyway," which reflect feelings of
hopelessness and helplessness.

The Disoriented. Disoriented people are apt to have delusions or hallucinations, and the suicidal danger is that they may
respond to commands, voices, or expressions that others cannot
share. When a disoriented person expresses suicidal notions, it is
important to consider this a most serious suicidal risk. Even
knowing where he or she is and what date it is does not rule out
disorientation regarding who he or she is, especially if asked
more or less "philosophic" questions, like What is the meaning
of life? The person's thinking will seem peculiar, and the words
will have some special or idiosyncratic characteristics.

The Defiant. Many individuals, no matter how miserable
their circumstances or how painful their lives, attempt to regain some shred of control over their own fate. Thus, a man
dying of cancer may choose to play one last active role in his
own life by picking the time of his death rather than passively
capitulating to the disease. Such a person is described as one
who has an active need to control his environment. Typically,
he would never be fired from any job; he would quit. In a
hospital he would attempt to control by refusing some treatments, demanding others, requesting changes, insisting on

Table 8.2
FACTORS ASSOCIATED WITH SUICIDAL RISK

---

1. **Age:** The rate for successful suicide increases with age though recent data indicate a marked increase in the suicide rate for young people (teens and early twenties). From 1965 to 1975, the number of suicides in the 20–24 age range more than doubled from 1400 to 3000.

2. **Sex:** Though women attempt suicide more often than men, men are more likely to be successful in their attempts, due in part to the use of more lethal means. After age 60, the gap for committing suicide between men and women narrows.

3. **Race:** The overall rate for whites is three times that among blacks, though among urban blacks (20–35 age range) the rate is twice that for whites of the same age. The rate for American Indians increased a marked 36 percent between 1970–1975. The rate for Indians in 1975 was 21.6 per 100,000 population, which is 70 percent higher than for all races, 64 percent higher than whites and 254 percent higher than blacks.

4. **Suicide Plan:** The more specific and concrete the plan for taking one's life, the greater the risk. An individual who has taken steps in preparation for death (changing a will, giving up cherished possessions, writing notes), has chosen a highly lethal method (guns, lethal dosage of pills, etc.), and has the means to carry out the plan (gun in possession, or pills in the medicine cabinet) is a much higher suicidal risk than an individual for whom suicide is still primarily a thought or fantasy.

5. **History of Previous Attempts:** The number of suicide attempts far outweigh the number of completed suicides in the United States, about 10 to 1 in adults, and 50 to 1 in adolescents. Suicidal risk increases as the number of attempts increases since individuals often choose more lethal means with subsequent attempts (guns, as opposed to taking pills or breathing gas with the chance of subsequent discovery). Increased risk is also associated with the increased possibility of dying by accident during a suicidal attempt.

6. **Social Supports and Resources:** Suicidal risk increases as social isolation increases—living alone or withdrawing from social contacts.

7. **Recent Loss:** Common precipitating events—losses—for suicide include death of a loved one; divorce or separation; loss of health through ill-

ness, accident or surgery; loss of job; or loss of self-esteem through threat of criminal prosecution.

8. **Emotional Symptoms:** The most common suicidal symptoms are related to depression (apathy and despondency, loss of appetite, weight loss, inability to sleep at night, loss of interest in social activities, and general physical and emotional exhaustion). Suicidal behavior may also be the result of psychotic states, for example, a patient acting on delusions, hallucinations, or other disorientation in time and place.

9. **Medical Problems:** The diagnosis of debilitating illness can affect both life style and self-image (breast cancer, loss of limb, heart disease), thereby heightening the risk of suicide. Physicians and other health care practitioners also see patients who present relatively minor physical complaints which actually mask depression or other psychological distress. If they do not inquire about life circumstances surrounding the physical complaint, health care practitioners may miss clues to possible suicidal ideation.

10. **Alcohol and Other Drugs:** Drinking increases suicidal risks since it increases impulsive behavior and reduces the number of pills necessary to make a dose lethal.

Source: From Karl A. Slaikeu, *Crisis Intervention: A Handbook for Practice and Research.* Copyright © 1984 by Allyn and Bacon, Inc. Reprinted with permission.

privileges—all indicating an inner need to direct and control his life situation. These individuals are seen as having low frustration tolerance, being fairly set in their ways, being somewhat arbitrary, and in general, showing a great oversensitivity to outside control.

The Dependent-Dissatisfied. Such an individual is very dependent on others, but simultaneously is dissatisfied with this dependency and the quality of help given him or her. Such individuals become increasingly tense and depressed, with frequent expressions of guilt and inadequacy. Alternatively, this individual rejects the people around him or her and denies feeling any need for help, then becomes overdemanding, insisting on help from those same people. Any suicide threats or attempts on the part of such persons, no matter how mild, may be real.

In conclusion, as long as suicidal individuals call out for help, there is a chance to save them. One of the more important aspects in helping suicidal individuals is personal warmth toward these individuals and the ability to arouse hope for the future. In the greatest number of actual suicides, there is no call for help and no way of knowing. The best one can do is to make these people realize that someone is there when they need a friend.

EMERGENCY PROCEDURES

In a crisis, the practitioner must be aware of entering someone's life at a critical time. In the normal course of life, it is difficult to tell another person about one's problems; at a time of a crisis, this process becomes even more difficult. Therefore, a trusting relationship must be formed. Being accepting and nonjudgmental are the first steps toward this very important relationship. Avoiding unnecessary questions and not giving advice usually is the best course of action. Sometimes, just listening to the person is more effective than trying to solve the problem. By allowing individuals to solve their own problems, the practitioner avoids dependency and increases the self-confidence necessary in regaining control over one's own life. The person in crisis needs someone who is positive and empathic in his or her responses, one who understands and gives reassurance that the problem can be resolved. Being empathic means listening to the individual, attempting to sincerely understand his or her problems and feelings regarding them. Empathic understanding is being able to put oneself in the other person's world, being able to sense how the individual feels, thinks, interprets, and reacts to the world.

Sometimes the situation may seem so critical that the practitioner fears expressing his or her anxieties about the crisis. This can escalate the crisis, since the person in crisis is calling for assistance and may sense the practitioner's panic. Remain calm, taking deep breaths to regain composure. A person who loses control is not in a position to help anyone. At other times during a crisis, the practitioner may draw a blank on how to respond to an individual. At these times, the practitioner should trust his or her own feelings. Be empathic: ask the question How would I feel? Another technique is to paraphrase what the individual has just said, reflecting his or her thoughts and feelings in order to communicate understanding of what the individual is saying. Being able to repeat back, in your own words, what the person has said will prove helpful, especially when these thoughts and feelings are expressed with the same intensity of emotion and in a manner that demonstrates a deep understanding of what was meant by them. Paraphrasing is a technique for obtaining more information about the situation and will encourage the individual to continue. It is most important to realize one's own limits in a crisis situation. If necessary, refer the individual to another professional with more experience.

PROBLEM SOLVING

Problem solving is perhaps the most important task of working with the emotionally disturbed individual. Ideally, practitioners have the ability to effectively cope with and address problems in their own lives and are able to share these skills with the emotionally disturbed individual. Solving problems is not easy and is even more difficult for the emotionally disturbed. Crises seem to happen more frequently with these individuals due to their inability to solve problems.

Effective problem solving is twofold: The first step is to resolve the immediate crisis. This requires intervention skills and an awareness of all the community resources available to accomplish this task. The next step, and perhaps the most important, is preventing problems from recurring through such methods as decision making, coping skills, and long-range planning. These skills form a pattern that helps prevent problems from recurring.

In order to avoid problems in the future, certain planning actions must be undertaken proactively by the individual needing assistance, such as determining long-term goals. In many cases, this is the most difficult aspect of problem solving, but deciding on a particular goal is the first step in reaching it. Even not making a decision is a decision, which perhaps is the most dangerous of all, because it leaves the individual totally unable to predict situations that will arise in the future. Therefore, setting a goal, deciding to move toward it, having the motivation to change, and obtaining the opportunity to do so are the essential elements to creatively progress through life.

Five interwoven components seem to play important roles in problem solving: (1) formulating the goal; (2) making the decision; (3) having the motivation for change; (4) having the opportunity for change; and (5) being creative in approaching the problem.

The Goal

Having a clear idea of what one wants is the first step in problem solving. In other words, what is the goal? What is the desired end? After this decision has been made, much of the planning process is complete, and what remains is simply and logically following a course of action or steps toward the goal.

The Decision

Action must follow conception of ideas; otherwise, the idea drifts off into dreamland. An idea that is not acted upon immediately may drift off and never be acted upon. To avoid losing a goal to inaction requires making decisions about how to reach the objective. The struggle to act seems to be just as important as the idea itself. Action brings life to an idea but requires the energy to act on the decision. What price is one willing to pay to achieve the goal? Everything costs, and if the cost is too high, then the idea probably will never come to pass. This decision is the basis of our motivation that moves people toward change.

Motivation

An important question to ask when working with someone in solving problems is Has this person the motivation to change? If there is no motivation, there will be no change. Most individuals are motivated to change their lives because of some aversion or discomfort. Rarely does a comfortable person want to change his or her life. The individual has to be motivated to work at changing the circumstances. Emotionally disturbed individuals are dependent and sometimes get angry because they want the practitioner to make their lives better. However, true change will occur only if the person is willing to change.

Opportunity

Opportunity is an important part of success, but not as important as one might think. People do not have to wait for opportunity to knock; they can proactively create the opportunity. Opportunity is all around all of the time and requires only the ability to see it and take advantage of it. Being prepared and establishing goals makes people aware of the opportunities around them, which is the best way to make things happen. Opportunity can be created by being prepared.

Creativity

A creative force also must be at play in problem solving. Many times, the practitioner does not have the answer at hand or the resources available to solve a problem. But, by creatively combining forces with other things that are similar and available, the solution to a problem can be created. Crises need to be solved immediately; one doesn't have the luxury of waiting for the right time and circumstances, and so creativity is required. But achieving long-term goals also takes a creative approach. Most problems can be solved if a goal is set, actions are planned, those involved are motivated, the opportunity to make it happen is sought, and the plans are put into action creatively.

FOLLOW-UP

Solving an immediate crisis does not prevent new crises from emerging. This takes work with the individual. Many times, the practitioner's first contact with an individual is during a state of crisis. Solving the current crisis is only the first step in the treatment of the whole individual. Follow-up care usually is necessary, as well as prudent to consider, when working with an individual in crisis. The aftermath of a crisis can be just as critical as the crisis itself. Therefore, encouraging follow-up treatment is recommended. It is always wise to have this available as an additional resource for the individual.

Too often practitioners feel satisfied with the successful resolution of the immediate crisis. They inadvertently forget about the individual until the next crisis emerges. This may be due to scarce resources or the increasing demands for service, but practitioners must consider the broader implications of their actions. Is the person returning to the same situation that first precipitated the crisis? Has anything changed within the individual other than having the immediate crisis resolved? Something, anything, must change within the individual as a result of intervention. The individual also must be aware of the change and understand it if there is to be a long-lasting solution.

Many cities have crisis centers. These emergency centers have been established as a social safety net for individuals in crisis, when there is nowhere else to turn. When there are no other alternatives for these individuals in crisis, the emergency centers take their calls for help.

Establishing a network of resources is extremely important for the crisis intervention worker. The network structure brings together all available community resources for solving a crisis. The issue then is one of referring the individual in crisis to the appropriate agencies. The professional has contacts and knowledge of all the community resources available, as well as how to get them to meet the individual needs of their clients. Knowing community resources can be the greatest asset in helping people in crisis.

Quick response to crises may be the difference between a life or death situation. Therefore, having a plan and being prepared are the most important components to resolving a crisis situation. It also is important to be aware of the signals that indicate that a crisis can develop into an explosive situation. It is much easier to intercede and solve a problem before it becomes a crisis, rather than afterward. By teaching prevention and problem solving, practitioners can bring about a radical decrease in the number of developing crises.

9. *Expect the Unexpected*
Special Topics

*T*his chapter provides some practical, how-to advice in dealing with a number of situations that inevitably occur in working with the emotionally disturbed. First of all, any serious or recurring problem always should be addressed with a treatment plan. Much thought and planning is necessary to change major difficulties. On the other hand, frequently events happen spontaneously and it is helpful to have some guidelines on how to respond effectively. The following suggestions are gathered from many of the reference sources listed elsewhere in this book. Additionally, these interventions are based on the authors' experiences with the emotionally disturbed. We have found the interventions to be both practical and effective. A word of caution: your particular needs and those of your program supervisors and fellow staff members obviously will be different from ours. You should discuss these suggested interactions with supervisors and other staff members. This will do two things. If all agree on these approaches you can feel free to use these interventions with the support of others. Also, it will facilitate discussion for additional or alternative ways of dealing with your specific situations and the populations that you work with.

DELUSIONS

It would seem that the way to expose false beliefs would be with cold, hard facts. However, factual explanations rarely, if

171

ever, convince a delusional person of the error of his or her thinking. Delusions are held onto because of emotional attachments, not rational decisions. Therefore, any attempt to change someone's delusional beliefs must take into account the influence of these emotional factors. However, during intervention, the practitioner should continue to point out that he or she sees things in a different way. For example, "I know that you believe it is this way, but I believe like this." With this approach, the effectiveness in reaching the delusional person will depend on how strongly that person trusts and values the practitioner's opinion.

Delusions, no matter how odd or strange, may have some basis in fact; at least some connection to reality is present in even the most bizarre story. The problem is that the person has misinterpreted or grossly expanded on minor points. Connections may have been made between things that were never meant to be connected. For example, one fellow frequently talked about sailing back to China. Of course, the fellow actually had never been to China, but he had grown up in a small city located in an area called China by most of the local residents. With this new knowledge it was clear that the desire to return to China was not so off the wall. Other people simply lacked all the pieces to the story. Even the most delusional ideas have some reference to facts.

A person who cannot accept or tolerate reality may change that reality to make it more possible to cope with. Over time, the emotionally disturbed person may trust the practitioner enough to give up the false beliefs. By asking a person to give up a delusional belief, one in effect is asking them to give up a source of security. Somehow the false belief has protected them against thoughts or feelings that could not be coped with in any other way. Although this mode of coping or "defense" cripples the ability to relate with others, it may be the only way that seems to work. Therefore, the emotionally disturbed person must have some other form of security or way of coping in return for giving up this particular delusional belief.

What is needed in treating delusional beliefs is emotional support. This type of trusting relationship will need time to develop and will take many interactions between staff members and the delusional individual. In the meantime, when faced with delusions, the person must know that staff members understand that the person believes in the delusion, even though they believe in something different. Do not accept the delusion, but try not to be too critical early on. Do not take too firm a stand against it. This will only strengthen the individual's feeling of isolation from others. Remember that this belief has developed over time so it will take time to change the person's delusional response habits. A person cannot be expected to relinquish delusions on the first encounter.

Another strategy is to tell these individuals that they can believe whatever they want to, but telling others in the community these strange or unfamiliar ideas will make their own lives more difficult because others are not likely to believe them. This could be stated as "some people are liable to tell you that your thinking is crazy." Continue by explaining that "it would be better for you to keep it to yourself or at least try to act normal, even if it is only an act." Another strategy is to ask the person if the belief leads him or her to feel better or makes life easier or more successful. If not, suggest that he or she try "acting" in a different manner. Even the person who continues to think or believe as before now has a way of "acting" that will reduce problems in getting along with others. Also, the person may be willing to discuss other alternative behavior after realizing that such beliefs make life more difficult or unproductive.

The interventions just suggested are only a few ways to work with delusional beliefs. Some mental health workers will discuss the delusional beliefs directly and in great depth with the person. This type of intervention requires a great deal of experience and a high level of skill. The interventions discussed in this section are brief and less complicated methods.

HALLUCINATIONS

People who report hearing voices or seeing things often find this an extremely frightening experience. It is something that they want to stop and prevent from ever happening again. On the other hand, some people consciously or unknowingly cultivate these odd sensations by paying close attention to the experience and thinking about it a great deal. Breaking through the attraction to an internal fantasy world is a difficult task. Practitioners must attempt to make the reality of everyday life more attractive than the retreat into fantasy. The people who experience hallucinations do so because they are extremely lonely and isolated. A strange voice may serve as a source of comfort and human contact, even though to most others this seems like a terribly unproductive way of relating.

People so wrapped up in their own thoughts that they seem to be responding only to some inner stimulus need immediate intervention. That is, speak to them or redirect them to the here and now. Calmly, yet firmly, provide alternatives such as chores or arts and crafts activities. Activity forces the person's thinking to be brought to the here and now because the body is acting in the here and now.

For those whose hallucinations are unpleasant or disturbing, staff members need to provide emotional support. Explain that the voices or sights are not real, but part of the emotional difficulties being coped with. Reassure them that the hallucinations will go away as they feel better about themselves.

Many who hear unpleasant voices report that the voices accuse them of thinking awful thoughts. Some relate that voices prod them to attempt unacceptable behaviors, such as killing themselves or harming loved ones. One theory is that the voices are caused by guilt: the person feels such overwhelming guilt that he or she begins to hear accusations. For this reason, the reassurance that voices will ease as the person feels better about himself or herself is logical.

It may seem obvious that such persons should try not to listen to what the voices say, but tell them not to listen anyway. Many are very unsure about the whole experience and may feel compelled to listen to "the voices." Remind them that they do not have to listen to or believe what is "said" to them. Also add that not listening or paying attention will help them reduce the frequency of the experience.

Since isolation and lack of human contact can lead to hallucinations, another effective intervention is to help the person build activities to fill idle time. Help them locate volunteer positions, hobbies, pastimes, or projects. They may need help in setting up a schedule with specific things to do at specific times. This type of planning is needed most over the weekends, especially if the program does not offer weekend services.

THE UNMOTIVATED INDIVIDUAL

Sam would not go to group sessions. Regardless of the subject the group discussed, he would refuse to attend and usually just sat in a corner. Most of the time he was pleasant in his refusal, but he would never join the group. After some time, the staff members stopped asking Sam to join the group or activities. Letting him sit in the corner was much easier because he was no problem. Some even thought, "Why bother him?" Over time, when working with the emotionally disturbed, there will be people who seem unmotivated to join, cooperate, or respond. Overworked staff members on a tight schedule sometimes are tempted to neglect such a person. Or worse, they may attempt to force a person into complying. Verbal hounding or physical prompting will create frustration in both the staff and the emotionally disturbed person. This type of intervention also borders on violating the person's rights.

Frequently, what may seem to be poor motivation in reality is the fear of failure. Most emotionally disturbed people have experienced many failures and losses: so much so, that they have come to expect failure and loss in their lives. These feelings are unpleasant for anyone, regardless of how frequent they are. Therefore, rather than fail, it is much easier not to try in the first place. If they knew in advance they were going to fail miserably, few people would attempt any activity. Poor motivation springs mostly from the fear of failure rather than lack of interest or plain laziness. Over time, this lack of response becomes a habit, a standard way of responding to all requests from others. The only way to reduce the risks for "unmotivated" persons is to ask them to do things both you and they know they can succeed in. However, do not go overboard. Be sure the person develops his or her own goals and does not fulfill only the expectations and goals of others. This process takes time, but opportunities will present themselves. In Sam's case, the group leader passed out materials to all the group members. She also placed some where Sam could see them without any effort. From time to time, subjects were discussed that Sam knew something about. The leader would ask for Sam's comments, and he would answer. So the milieu, or the total program, was successful in getting Sam to join the group without forcing him to move. The group met Sam on his own terms.

Remember, liberally praise attempts as well as successes. As stated previously, poor motivation really is more like fear or panic than laziness. Tell the person that he or she will be safe. Explain that help is available, and that he or she will not die or be harmed by taking some type of action. Be reasonable in this reassurance. Do not make promises that cannot be delivered. Take time to let others know that you are interested in them even if you are not sure what they may be going through. Admit that you do not know for sure what they may be thinking or feeling but that you are interested if they care to share anything. Be patient. Any relationship takes time to develop.

THE AGGRESSIVE INDIVIDUAL

The aggressive individual screams, breaks things, fights, and may use weapons. The presence of any of these activities renders a program less effective because both staff member and clients are frightened. The concern will center on physical safety rather than on developing skills and solving problems. Under such conditions no other work or progress will take place. Obviously, the threat of violence must be removed. To effectively deal with aggressive acts the staff members must get across the message that such behavior will not be allowed in the treatment setting. One way to get across this idea is to post house rules and clearly label all unacceptable acts, including violent acts. Additionally, and equally important, staff members must also get across the idea that anger and frustration are legitimate feelings and can be expressed properly. All feelings are natural. Angry feelings are natural. Although feelings at times are difficult to contain, people can control the way they behave and the way they act. Frequently, practitioners are tempted to use the words *appropriate* and *inappropriate* when describing behaviors, but these words should be used carefully. When a person loses control of angry feelings, it is much more appropriate to scream than to break something or hurt somebody. Therefore, be careful in telling someone who is screaming that the behavior is not appropriate. Be careful not to take away their only way of expressing what they feel. Aggressive acts tend to flow when people feel they have lost their usual avenues for coping. Always give the potentially violent person a chance to ventilate his or her feelings by talking. Suggest they begin talking with "I am so mad at . . ." or "what makes me angry is. . . ." Suggest exercises or walking. If possible, guide them to a different room or area, but always try to avoid physically cornering a person. A cornered person has nothing to lose by acting violently. If the person will go, take a walk. This is one of the best alternatives. Perhaps the change in the environment will change the perception of the need for violence. Possibly, it will provide chances for alternative behavior. Walking away also provides a person a chance to "save face" in front of their peers.

Should a violent act occur, staff members need to be in control of the situation. People attending a program need to know that program staff will not allow physical harm to result from someone temporarily losing control. If a person is totally out of control, the police may have to be called. There should be a prearranged procedure for contacting other staff members for assistance; a code word or phrase immediately lets others know that their assistance is needed, that an emergency situation is in progress. If possible, remove other people from the area, since an audience tends to escalate the issue.

Since violent acts are a possibility, all staff members should be trained in therapeutic physical intervention. These are methods of physically restraining people from hurting themselves or others. Physical intervention should be used rarely and only as a last resort. The reader is encouraged to take this recommendation seriously. Generally, overuse of physical intervention by staff members promotes violence in others; that is, one behavioral outburst tends to incite others to follow suit. Our experience has been that the best intervention is to get across the message that violence is taboo and that other ways to express feelings can and must be found. Again, physical intervention should be used only when there is danger to the physical safety of others or the risk of damage to property. However, do not be overly concerned with damage to property. Most things can be replaced. Harm to people must be avoided in all cases. Talk about these kinds of procedures at staff meetings and decide ahead of time what to do if someone should lose control and become aggressive.

NONCOMPLIANCE

Noncompliance is a different form of "lack of motivation." The person is doing something, but it is not what you want him or her to do. Under these circumstances, the person is not only resisting what the practitioner says but may be doing the opposite. Some emotionally disturbed people have been in hospitals for long periods of time, perhaps many, many years. They have been in an environment where they were told what to do, when to eat, when to get up, when to come and go, and so on. They had little control over their lives in this setup. The final shred of control that remained was whether to cooperate or not. Being resistive or noncompliant is really a struggle over control.

Staff members must avoid power struggles at this point. Avoid making ultimatums. Avoid win or lose situations. In the end, staff members always lose. Even if the staff person succeeds in forcing a person to comply, the damage done to the relationship amounts to a loss. Although the person may be forced into a specific action, trust and cooperation cannot be forced, and probably will not be forthcoming for a very long time. Try giving a resistive person two or more alternatives from which to pick. Someone who is given an alternative has a choice or at least some control over what happens. If possible, do not make doing nothing or resisting one of the alternatives. However, if the person chooses to do nothing, the response should be, "Alright, it is your choice to leave this group," or

"You are choosing to do. . . ." Even though the battle may seem to be lost, the practitioner has begun to give the person control over his or her life. On other occasions, this may open the door for a conversation with the person, in which the practitioner explains, "I did not like the choice that you made, but it is important that you made a choice." Allowing people choices and control over their lives will make them less defensive or resistive to further intervention.

Related to noncompliance is the case of the person who refuses to receive needed treatment. Of course, each case must be dealt with as circumstances require, but considered here are some responses to the person who will not participate.

Assertive Intervention

This can mean frequent contact with the person's place of residence. Home visits or, certainly, telephone calls should be attempted. In this situation, the practitioner must weigh the negative aspects of intruding on someone's privacy against the seriousness of the disturbance before deciding on a course of action.

Contact with Significant Others

Family members, friends, and lovers may be able to persuade the person to attend treatment or they can serve as a contact source. Confidentiality is a primary concern, but in crisis situations, confidentiality may need to be breached in order to react effectively and appropriately.

Involuntary Hospitalization

Each state has a mental health code that outlines the circumstances and procedures for involuntary hospitalization. This is a serious step, but occasionally it is a necessary one. Court-ordered attendance at a program may be the result.

Personal Rights

Ultimately, people have the right to decide against treatment. Despite unusual thinking or behavior, people must be allowed to make decisions, even if they lead to mistakes. Perhaps the best that can be done in some cases is letting the person know what services are available.

SEXUAL ACTIVITIES

When people are together long enough, there is the potential for sexual attraction and sexual activity, whether the people are emotionally disturbed or not. Instead of saying that sex is bad or shameful, practitioners who view themselves as enlightened often tell people that "sex is okay, but not here in the program—this is not the time or the place." Unfortunately, people in programs may never get to see each other elsewhere. This presents a dilemma.

Everyone has ideas about what is right and wrong, and staff members will have to come to an agreement about what they feel the program can tolerate comfortably. When dealing with those who are involved sexually, practitioners have to emphasize responsible behavior, both public and private. Emphasis should be placed on intimate feelings and closeness and a perception of sex as much more than fulfilling biological drives and needs. Discussions about love and emotional unity and companionship are useful and need attention.

If two people have acted responsibly and now indicate that they would like to extend this relationship to the sexual area, staff members can provide useful counseling. A natural starting point is to have the people consider birth control. Particularly for an emotionally disturbed woman, pregnancy will add a number of obstacles and she is likely to face a difficult and demanding situation in the future. People may already think of her as incompetent. Additionally, if she is taking medication, she would be taken off that medicine for the health of the infant. Finally, she would be subject to frequent advice and criticism.

Staff members have a responsibility to give the people they work with information they need to make informed decisions. As we all know, people will have sexual contact. Whether sexual contact should be allowed within a program is partly an ethical decision. But, whatever the decision, providing education about feelings, biology, and sexuality is a responsibility that staff members should take on for the people that they serve. If sexual activity is not to be allowed, the staff members must decide how to enforce such a rule. On the other hand, if staff members feel that such behavior could be allowed, when and where sexual activities are appropriate and what constitutes a sexual activity need consideration. Perhaps those who are sexually involved can be helped to make arrangements for getting together on dates or outings outside of program hours.

FAMILIES

Sadly, families have had to accept much of the blame for emotionally disturbed offspring. Even though the children are now adults, family members feel guilty and frustrated about producing a "sick" child. This feeling of blame can be heightened by staff members who firmly support the idea that emotional disturbance is a by-product of faulty upbringing. A family that feels accused and guilty very likely will be reluctant to support treatment. This is a tragic situation. A family should not have to shoulder the total blame for the poor decisions of an emotionally disturbed offspring.

Family members spend more time and have a greater overall stake in the welfare of an emotionally disturbed person than other people, including practitioners. Family members sometimes can reach a person more effectively than an outsider, such as a counselor. Families will need education about the causes of emotional disturbance. They also need to know how to manage interactions with their emotionally disturbed relative.

Families frequently find it difficult to come in for "therapy" sessions. If such is the case, they may need a way to save face and still be given information. We have found two ways to do this. One is by using recreational activities such as picnics, holiday parties, or open houses. Families can come to the treatment setting during this nonthreatening occasion. Initial contacts can be made and later drawn upon for additional therapy at a future time.

The second effective strategy is to hold didactic groups, that is, teaching sessions on topics of general interest. A good starting point for these groups is the uses and limits of medication. Often, if the family understands what medicine can and cannot do, the members will become allies in getting the emotionally disturbed person to take the prescribed medication. Other topics to include in these groups might be behavior modification, available services and benefits for the emotionally disturbed, crisis intervention and support systems, and hospitalization and the involuntary petitioning process. One of the biggest mistakes made in treatment is neglecting the power of the family.

BASEBALL THERAPY

Another myth of emotional disturbance is that people suffering with these problems are total wrecks. In nearly every case, the people are quite skilled and capable in other areas of their lives. The practitioner's job is to find these interests or talents and expand upon them. Capitalizing on people's skills and strengths will enhance self-esteem and shore up their overall good feelings about themselves. They may even feel secure enough in themselves to take risks in other areas. Athletics and games are excellent ways of building new roles. Frequently, emotionally disturbed people see themselves as "mentally ill"; everything they do is colored by this perception. They need to experience for themselves another role. Team sports like softball, volleyball, or doubles ping-pong, are a great source of new roles. It is hard to maintain the role of a mentally ill person while you are in the role of a shortstop, a spiker, or a server. It is amazing the skills that some people will display.

A word of caution: it is important to find a method of choosing teams that does not leave the worst player chosen last. The pain and rejection felt in the second grade over being picked last can still be relived. Get everybody involved. Even if some insist that they cannot play, have them keep score, keep time, or keep track of who should be where.

A second word of caution: if a game is played outside, always provide plenty of water and sunscreen and encourage liberal use of both. Many antipsychotic medications have side effects that include hypersensitivity to the sun; that is, people taking these medications are more susceptible to heatstroke or sunburn. Some medications impair the body's ability to regulate heat and additional protection is wise. Activities in general will provide all sorts of opportunities to hand out encouragement and recognition. Group members also may benefit from the camaraderie that goes with being part of a team or a group. And, of course, the benefits of exercise go without saying. Lastly, the experience of having fun is valuable. Many emotionally disturbed people seem to have lost the ability to laugh and enjoy themselves. Games and activities help redevelop these feelings.

BORROWING, LENDING, EXTORTING

Since many emotionally disturbed people are not working, temporarily or permanently, money usually is tight. Even though they may receive benefits, their funds typically will be almost totally absorbed by room and board. Subsequently, extra items such as cigarettes, coffee, or soda pop can become luxuries. As such, people without these luxuries will try to obtain them. This leads to problems of borrowing, lending, and extorting. Of course, these practices should be discouraged or banned. Again, when there are house rules, this may be added to them. Typically, however, banning such practices is easier said than done. Many people are afraid of others, are afraid of reprisal, or are afraid of being disliked. They may feel that by saying no they will lose affection or friendship. Unfortunately, this penalizes those who economically save their own money for their own goods. Others who have used up their own money will badger those who have not. Staff members must make such badgering one of those forbidden practices, like fighting or violence. Beyond this, practitioners must empower clients by telling them that it is alright to say no and help them make up reasons for saying no if they cannot think of any on their own. Remember, those with newly developed assertive skills may need assistance until they have enough confidence to deal with "moochers." The opposite end of this strategy is working with the "moochers," helping them develop a budget. Helping some-

one devise a budget will not only eliminate the problem of
frequent borrowing but also will provide an invaluable daily
living skill. If you can find a way to help someone stretch a
paycheck from one payday to the next, please spread the word
so everyone, including staff members, can learn that special
skill!

ODDS AND ENDS

What follows are some brief tips or guidelines that did not
seem to fit anywhere else.

Nonresponse and Awareness

Sometimes the emotionally disturbed person will withdraw
into a personal world and refuse to respond to others. Neither
verbal nor written communication seems to penetrate the wall
of nonresponsiveness. The person seems to be totally cut off
from others. In reality, however, the withdrawn person is very
aware of what is happening. This is shown clearly when, after
improvement, the person explains, "I remember what was going on. I just couldn't respond at the time." So, be aware that
such people do pick up what is said. Emotionally disturbed
people have spent a lifetime monitoring what others think,
feel, and say. Even though they may misinterpret or distort,
they are quite aware of what is going on, even when they are in
seemingly nonresponsive states.

Do not talk about somebody who is present in a room as if
that person were not there. People may be disturbed or acting
in a bizarre manner, but at some level, they are always aware of
what is going on. They tune in even though it may seem that
they are "out of it." People know what is said or at least they
will be aware of how they are being treated.

Eye Contact

When addressing somebody, sit or stand at the person's eye
level. This is a common courtesy, which shows concern and
interest. It probably is not on a conscious level; however, all of
us feel more comfortable and willing to open up to someone

who looks us in the eye. This minor act also helps remove the "we staff—you patient" status that tends to be overemphasized at times. Of course, there are actual differences in status, and these can be used to advantage in treatment, but keep aware of the potential for problems. People who feel they are being "looked down on" will soon begin to act and feel that they are not as worthy as the staff.

Religion

People often are tortured by thoughts of God and their own guilt. They may feel that they are being punished or deserve to be severely punished for real or imagined transgressions. Discussing theology or religion tends to lead into conflicts or bizarre, delusional talk from a person so religiously preoccupied.

Many people have deeply held religious beliefs and thoughts. We feel it is best to simply state that God is good and would never torture or harm someone for mistakes they have made. Perhaps you could explain to them that your belief is that God is good and God would like to be a help and a source of strength for them. If you are tempted to immediately dismiss someone's religious beliefs, stop. Labeling another person's beliefs as unworkable or unusable will cut off communication. The chances of reopening communication then will be severely hampered.

Magical Thinking

Some emotionally disturbed people believe that if you think about something, it will come true. The formal name for this thinking process is *magical thinking*. This type of thinking produces much guilt if a person wishes something bad to happen to someone and by coincidence or by inevitability something bad does happen to that person. For example, Elizabeth talked about hating her mother. She spoke of how she wished that her mother would die and leave her alone. Her mother was involved in a car accident and was seriously injured. For a long period afterward, Elizabeth was bothered by the thought that her desire to have her mother die or be gone had in fact resulted in her mother's auto accident. If this subject does come up, tell the person that "thinking does not make it so." Thoughts and feelings are spontaneous and difficult to control but behavior can be controlled. For people who tend to believe in magical thinking, the point must be made that simply thinking about something does not make it happen.

Response Time

Some emotionally disturbed people seem to take forever to respond. It is as if they have not heard anyone or do not care to respond. Usually, the opposite is the case. Be patient and give them time to respond. It may take thirty seconds, or one minute, or longer. If they never respond verbally, tell them that you will be back, then leave, but return later and wait for a response again. This will convey concern and interest. Gradually, the person may feel secure enough to venture a response to you.

This chapter provided a few suggestions that may be useful in specific situations. Some of the interventions are unexpected, but much useful therapy is based on clear thinking and common sense. As such, most specific situations can be dealt with by a person that takes time to plan. As previously stated, all behavior has meaning. A practitioner needs to find out what a symptom means or what a person receives from a specific behavior. Once this is determined, then it is possible to plan a treatment intervention that can have some chance for success.

10. *What Am I Doing Here?*
Practitioners

*T*hroughout this book, the focus has been primarily on emotionally disturbed individuals, the reactions to them by society, and various methods of treatment. All of these factors eventually take their toll on the practitioner. In view of this, attention now is turned to the issue of burnout. Later in this chapter, various job possibilities in the field will be discussed, as will the reasons why practitioners in the field of mental health are such special people.

BURNOUT

Causes and Symptoms

All people seem to be susceptible to burnout. Over time, burnout seems to slowly drain people of their energy and enthusiasm. They become bored with their jobs and can become ineffective in their work. In the helping professions, burnout has many causes. Too many clients for too few practitioners, long hours, and limited resources all contribute to burnout. In addition, disturbed individuals can be emotionally demanding and draining; they can be very dependent and in tremendous need of emotional fulfillment. Many such people are constantly attempting to fill their own emotional void, thereby depleting practitioners of their personal emotional reservoir. Therefore, it is important to realize how easily practitioners can fall into the trap of allowing the emotionally disturbed individual to become too dependent. These factors are difficult to control and resolve in themselves but, fortunately, are not the primary cause of burnout. Burnout can be controlled and prevented through an awareness of its symptoms and causes.

The symptoms of burnout (Welch, Medeiros, & Tate, 1982, pp. 21–43) manifest themselves in all aspects of people's lives, physically, intellectually, emotionally, socially, and spiritually. Physically, fatigue and exhaustion are the first symptoms of burnout. A burned-out person has little energy to move through life, and a night's sleep does not refresh the person's body and mind. In addition, the things that used to provide nutritional, physical, intellectual, or social enjoyment and relaxation lose their appeal. The person increasingly becomes frustrated, bored, disappointed, and angry. Intellectually, thinking clearly and quickly becomes difficult. Problems that once were easy to solve become difficult and time-consuming; those that were challenging become hopeless. Emotionally, there is nothing. In order to fill this emotional void and give some meaning to life, the burned-out person shifts all of his or her energy into the job. This overinvestment of energy leaves very little for the outside interests that could relax and refresh the individual. Socially, the individual begins feeling isolated from others, rather than involved and belonging. There is a marked decrease in the individual's ability to enjoy life. The person no longer seeks the company of others but tends to withdraw socially. The individual loses the social support that can help heal and resolve feelings of isolation. Spiritually, a void encompasses the individual's life as he or she realizes that personal expectations will never be fulfilled. Hence, life loses all its meaning.

Paramount to the prevention of burnout is understanding the role our personal expectations play in this process. Are the practitioner's expectations of success for the emotionally disturbed individual realistic? Are the goals established jointly with the individual attainable? What is the personal motivation for entering a "helping" field? Hundreds of other factors also have an impact on determining who will survive this very demanding line of work.

Burnout is paradoxical in that it seems to happen more often and more quickly to those with the greatest investments in their work, those most committed to doing whatever they can to assist the emotionally disturbed person. These individuals are most likely to be highly idealistic, enthusiastic, and hard working: the first to come up with an innovative solution to a problem, the last to give up on a difficult person. The characteristics are not the problem; in fact, they are necessary to work successfully in this field. The concern, therefore, is the motivation and perception behind these characteristics. If practitioners have unrealistic expectations or do not realize and accept the limitations of the individuals they treat, they soon begin setting themselves up for frustration and burnout.

Part of the problem of burnout is the belief that it is possible to "cure" emotionally disturbed individuals. Unfortunately, at this time, no one has a "cure" for these shattering disorders. Believing in such a cure impedes the realistic assessment of the individual's functioning level. This unrealistic perception, coupled with the pressure to produce results and normalization, can lead to eventual frustration and burnout. It places stress and pressures on the practitioner to help the emotionally disturbed individual improve. Of course, practitioners should work to the best of their abilities to help clients achieve their maximum functioning levels. But they must recognize that in some individuals progress is slow, and they should accept any progress as success. In order to appreciate the real progress that a disturbed individual has made, it is helpful to compare the person's level of functioning when entering care and what it is like now. The goal must be the restoration of a realistic level of functioning for the person and improving the quality of life.

Reflecting upon the realistic limitations of the emotionally disturbed means coming to terms with the question What is the most this person can become? Realistically, these individuals suffer from a number of major disabilities. Many do not possess the necessary vocational or social skills to be integrated readily into society and may require a sheltered living and working situation for the rest of their lives. Emotionally disturbed individuals are dependent and also particularly susceptible to stress. These stress symptoms are manifested in their inability to enjoy life. Having poor communication skills also results in the inability to build support systems. It is important for the practitioner to develop rapport and give social support to these

190 Practice, or How It Is Done

individuals. Setting realistic long-term goals along with attainable short-term objectives can be productive for the emotionally disturbed and gratifying for the practitioners, thus preventing burnout.

On the Job

Sometimes, it is helpful to recognize the symptoms of distress in colleagues and to offer some insight as to its prevention and treatment. It is easy to recognize burnout among the members in an organization:

> Perhaps some of the commonest symptoms of burnout are an increase in either formal or informal gatherings where the primary focus is one of complaints and dissatisfaction with the clients or the system in which they are working. This is a way of distancing oneself away from the clients who are likely to be a source of frustration that they are experiencing. The clients are likely to become the brunt of staff jokes which are cynical or sarcastic in nature. These are particularly directed at the perceived unresponsive client and are likely to be the recipients of much anger and resentment. The commonest process is the use of labeling as a distancing device, that is, calling the client names like "old crank, sociopath, hypochondriac, big-baby," et cetera. It is not unlikely that negative consequence is followed in the therapeutic relationship which is on a downward spiral for both the client and the staff member. (Mora, 1982, p. 101)

A true culprit in burnout is the way emotionally disturbed individuals are perceived and sometimes even the way they perceive themselves. This has been characterized by Steiner (1974), in the concept of the "rescue game." The game begins with the misperception that any person coming for advice or assistance is helpless in handling his or her own life, so helpless that one must intervene immediately to save them. Practitioners immediately come to the person's rescue: consciously because it's their job or unconsciously, perhaps, to meet their own needs. By acting to rescue them, these practitioners confirm the individual's feelings of powerlessness and helplessness. Thus, they continue to foster the dependency, making the individual more helpless and less confident to handle his or her own life. This leads to an inevitable vicious circle of helplessness, dependency, and powerlessness.

> Frequently, these rescuers are likely to experience a sense of bottomless responsibility and perhaps a great deal of heartache, frustration, and eventual failure. Therefore, working under these conditions fosters negative, persecutory attitudes about the people that you are needing to work with. . . . We become not their rescuer but their prosecutor, non-verbally saying that you are hopeless and helpless and its all your fault. "You are a bad patient." "I will no longer invest in you." Clearly then the feelings attached to this role are those of anger and hostility. (Mora, 1982, pp. 99–106)

Obviously, this game does not work, and the message of helplessness is not what one wants to convey to emotionally disturbed individuals. Practitioners hope to make these individuals more powerful and more in control of their personal lives. They must encourage the building of self-esteem and the growth of confidence through successfully handling life. They must realize that taking a chance on the clients' failure also means taking a chance on their success.

Ways of Preventing Burnout

Having realistic expectations of the abilities both of practitioners and their clients helps preserve emotional stability in the helping professions for years to come. Practitioners who want to avoid burnout can work at retaining the realistic outlook that preserves their satisfaction with their jobs. The following suggestions will prove helpful in making jobs more interesting, stimulating, and fulfilling, as well as in preventing burnout.

1. Have a good mixture of individuals in each caseload, individuals with various problems and capabilities. This will provide variety and stimulation. Where one individual fails, another may will succeed, creating a balance.
2. Have good supervision and talks with colleagues. These people can provide needed support and ideas that view problems in a new light.
3. Realize the importance of "down time," to allow practi-

tioners to replenish themselves. Inservice training sessions
or vacations will help to meet this need.

4. Avoid overinvolvement in work situations. Limit the
   amount of commitment to the job and the pressure accepted from it.
5. Accept the limitations of disturbed individuals and work
   with them in a realistic way.
6. Avoid dependency. Let individuals have the power to control their own lives. This is the only way they will be able to
   rebuild their personal self-esteem and self-worth.
7. Form treatment plans jointly with individuals, having them
   give you their commitment to the plan.
8. Focus and build on the individuals' strengths to reinforce
   their behavior and improve their self-esteem.
9. Provide support so that you can limit crises yet avoid
   overdependency.
10. Involve other staff members to limit the amount of depen-
    dency on any one individual.
11. Alter the job in some way when you need a change to keep
    work stimulating.
12. Socialize with other staff members outside working hours.
    Do things as a team. Have a potluck dinner, go on a picnic,
    or organize a party. A harmonious staff is an extremely
    important component in any therapeutic setting.

In order to continue working in this field for any length of
time, it is important to take care of oneself, both professionally
and personally. A practitioner's personal life helps replenish
his or her resources to come back to work refreshed and creative. People work for their entire lives, and, to ensure a high-
quality existence, they must feel good about themselves and
what they do. As in everything, they should strive to be the
very best they can be and *enjoy!*

JOB POSSIBILITIES

Settings

Where can someone equipped with knowledge about working with the emotionally disturbed find a job? What types of

settings use practitioners? What qualifications are needed for each of these positions? Today, the practitioner has many options from which to choose in the job market. Each position can be quite different, but most are stimulating and serve the needs of people who need support and help. Unfortunately, wages tend to be relatively modest; however, the experience and personal growth that can be gained while working with the emotionally disturbed can be rewarding and personally fulfilling. Some of the places that commonly utilize a practitioner's skills include the following.

Hospitals. These may be private local hospitals or state-operated institutions. Aides are used to staff three shifts per day, every day of the year. Hospital inpatient units, while considered the most restrictive setting, serve the broadest range of symptomatic conditions.

Day Treatment Centers and Partial Day Programs. People who have been discharged from a hospital but continue to need daily structure, activities, and further skill building often will be referred to a day program. Practitioners may assist or, in many cases, lead groups in this type of setting. This is a more typical 9 to 5 routine, although some programs may include weekends or evening sessions.

Group Homes. Some individuals who attend day programs also need a supervised living situation. Group homes provide this service and the direct care staff is composed almost exclusively of practitioners. Like a hospital, the group home has three shifts a day all year round.

Crisis Centers. Most communities that provide mental health services also have a crisis center. Practitioners may answer the crisis telephone lines, give referrals for needed services, or serve as brief counselors.

Domestic Assault Centers. The heightened awareness of the frequency and severity of family violence and sexual assault has meant the development of more and more shelters to house those subjected to violence. Practitioners are needed to assist in running the shelters and helping the victims plan their next action.

Work Activity Centers. These centers are similar to day treatment programs but focus on vocational placement and building job-related skills. A typical example is Goodwill Industries. Practitioners are needed to supervise the training of work skills and to see that production schedules are met.

Substance Abuse Clinics. These centers may provide information and referral for counseling or they may provide the counseling on site.

Other possible employment opportunities can be found at nursing homes, state social services departments, Social Security offices, or public education facilities.

Although there are differences in what will be expected of practitioners in different treatment settings, typically the job descriptions might look like this for a hospital practioner, or a day-program practioner. A typical day for a practitioner working on a psychiatric hospital unit would include some of the following duties:

1. Patient Count: a general accounting of the current whereabouts and activities of all people admitted to the unit.
2. Taking Vital Signs: recording the temperature, pulse, respiration, and blood pressures of patients.
3. Charting: recording vital signs and verbal and behavioral activity of patients. This may be a regular, standard procedure or done only for significant events related to specific goals.
4. Admissions: this may include checking all clothing and personal items that come into the unit. Most inpatient units have specific items that are prohibited for safety reasons, for example, glass items, sharp objects, and spray cans. This also may mean greeting and providing a general orientation for newly admitted patients and their families. These duties also may be repeated for people returning from outside.
5. Unit Monitoring: this may include talking and interacting with people on the unit. It also may take the form of checking for unlocked doors or taking inventory of supplies.

Each hospital will have specific job descriptions. Some will place greater responsibilities on their practitioners than others. Regardless of their duties each staff member has a specific role to carry out and efficient, responsible staff members make the difference in the effectiveness of any mental health program.

The job responsibilities of a practitioner in a community mental health day program might look like this:

1. Transportation: this involves driving the program's vehicle to pick up people coming into the program or taking them home at the end of the program day. In most cases a special driver's license is required.
2. Group Facilitation: leading groups in such diverse activities as education, recreation, or arts and crafts.
3. Teaching Daily Living Skills: this can be on a group or individual basis. These skills include money management, hygiene improvement, and interpersonal relations.
4. Record Keeping: observing and recording interactions and behavior of program participants. The point of this activity is to maintain a record of progress toward goals and a record of all services and treatment planning.
5. Observations: not only for record keeping but to assist the program physician in watching for medication side effects.
6. Program Participation: this includes attendance at staff meetings, inservice training sessions, and treatment development meetings.

Job Requirements

Staff members often do not need previous experience, but some minimal qualifications and required skills often are expected. Good physical health is a high priority, since active participation in treatment activities or program-related activities is expected. Good verbal skills are helpful, since many positions will require good speaking and listening skills. Formal education often is required. This may range from a minimum of a high school diploma, to an associate's degree, up to a completed bachelor's degree. Some settings even consider those with master's degrees as paraprofessionals. However, in most cases, a master's degree is not needed for employment as a paraprofessional practitioner. Experience always is helpful, but more and more, those who develop services are realizing that people with warmth, caring, and commitment can reach others in emotional pain. While training is essential, a doctorate is not always needed in order to be of assistance to others.

In general, employers in the mental health field look for practitioners who display good verbal and written skills, some knowledge of recreational techniques and practices, the ability to communicate with mentally dysfunctional people, the capacity to work well with other staff members, and the ability to accept supervision.

The ability to accept supervision is an important point. Even the most experienced worker needs supervision. Often other staff members can provide feedback or alternative approaches when one feels stuck or ineffective. All people feel frustrated when clients do not seem to improve. Therefore, supervision is vital not only in providing new ways to look at a problem, but also in giving each practitioner encouragement when treatment is not going as well as planned.

As in any other field of employment, finding a job in a mental health facility may require some ingenuity and persistence. Some people start as an unpaid volunteer and work their way into a paid position. Some facilities seek employees through newspaper ads. The local Community Mental Health Administration can tell a practitioner who to contact about a position. Someone already working in the field may be able to suggest a place that needs a practitioner. Make contacts with people in the field. It may not lead to a job right away but perhaps the person will consider you for an opening later on.

Consider taking part-time positions. Take a class that requires an internship or a field placement. Most programs are quite open to student placements. This, at least, will make you known to staff and possibly lead to employment.

Good luck, and try not to be discouraged if you do not land a position right away. Chances are that if you are the type of person that is willing to hang in there, some supervisor will recognize this quality and give you the chance to prove yourself.

PRACTITIONERS ARE SPECIAL

Delusional, disoriented, disinterested, disruptive, discharged—this was the description of an individual recently released from a state hospital and referred to a day program. The program was to accept this individual and assist him in getting his life back together. Of course, all the staff members screamed and moaned about this most recent referral but, as always, they accepted the individual into the program and began the long process of getting to know him.

Practitioners who work in the field of mental health are amazing people. It is no wonder that people in other fields often ask Why should anyone want to spend time working with crazy people? or How do you keep from going crazy yourself? These are good questions; they recognize that people do not go into this kind of work for the same reasons that they might become auto mechanics or legal secretaries.

The question then arises, Is a certain type of person attracted to this kind of work? There is no easy answer, because diversity appears to be the norm. A good treatment team is an association of all sorts of men and women, respecting each other for the individual contribution each is able to make. The staff of one center included several college dropouts, stuffy suburban housewives, nonstuffy suburban housewives, black labor leaders, an ex-nun, an ex-teacher, ex-drug users, and of course, pipe-smoking psychologists. The important thing is that they all worked together, according to their own talents and limitations.

Diverse as these individuals might seem, each primarily was on a personal quest. We have never met anyone in this profession who, in one way or another, was not dealing with his or her own private understanding of human hope and despair. The intensity of this work, the constant facing of defeat without becoming personally defeated, and the search for some way to redefine a situation to include the possibility of hope is an exhausting personal encounter.

Practitioners do not wish to see themselves as being like the individuals they treat. It is too painful. The psychotic individual frequently is so disturbed that he or she barely seems human. This individual often presents material in its rawest and least socially acceptable form. However, as has been explained, this is no accident. It is designed to frighten and "gross out" the practitioner. If the disturbed individual can offend and frighten others, those others become, in effect, allies in maintaining the psychotic adjustment. People will avoid an individual who frightens and offends them; this is a natural reaction. Thus, the psychotic individual once again has isolated himself or herself from people. Because people are frightened, they stop reaching out and begin treating the individual as different and strange—thus maintaining the psychotic adjustment.

When these situations occur, practitioners may feel overwhelmed. Their own defenses are under stress. They must be able to retreat sometimes. No one can work with emotionally disturbed individuals all day long, 365 days a year. The working life of a practitioner must include times of rest and reflection. Otherwise, they get burned out, permanently turned off, from too much coping.

People who are really effective in this work are able to keep going because they see it as part of their own development, not only professionally, but personally. Many people in this line of work have had their own brush with emotional problems— either in themselves, a relative, close friend, or in the way they look at the world—and are trying to view their work experience through a window that sometimes turns into a mirror (Beels, 1978, p. 281). The practitioner who is a seeker, who is not afraid to look inward, is an asset to most therapeutic communities. Knowing oneself leads to understanding, and thus helping, many others. Knowing oneself well, being comfortable with who one is and not being afraid or ashamed of limitations and weaknesses, makes one flexible and open to new experiences and ideas. The individuals with whom a practitioner works can, at times, be extremely disturbing to his or her own emotional makeup. We hope that this book has offered some guidelines and ideas about how to deal most effectively with this disturbing population.

As a final note, not only must all those in the field of mental health be educated and concerned about the emotionally disturbed, it also is their duty to educate the public. Many people still are frightened by the emotionally disturbed. Many see individuals with emotional problems as dangerous and threatening. Others, as strange as it may seem, still see the emotionally disturbed as being possessed by evil spirits. Still others discriminate against the emotionally disturbed and will laugh at, take advantage of, or even do violence to them.

Those who work in the field of mental health are the new leaders in this final revolution of educating the public about the emotionally disturbed. They must convey the message that emotionally disturbed individuals are perhaps the most vulnerable individuals in society today. To discriminate against these individuals is a crime and a reflection of an uneducated mentality. It is true that some emotionally disturbed individuals can be very frightening, although this is just their attempt to keep people away. Emotionally disturbed individuals have been hurt throughout their entire lives and do not want to be hurt again. Their symptoms are ingenuously designed to maintain the isolation, thus keeping them free from harm. It is a crime if the uneducated public harms these vulnerable individuals with cruel and spiteful actions.

It takes very special people to work in this most important and challenging field, especially at a time in history when many important changes and developments are occurring in the area of mental health. Those who work in this field are very unique and special people. For the most part, they are warm, caring, giving, and honest individuals concerned about the human condition, life, and the continued improvement of humanity. Most of all, it is important that such people recognize that they need to take of themselves, in order to take care of others. Practitioners are special people.

GLOSSARY

Acceptance: Recognition of an individual's worth without implying either approval of conduct or emotional attachment.

Acting Out: An active rather than a verbal response to an unconscious instinctual drive or impulse that brings about relief of inner tension.

Adjustment: Adaptation to society and to one's inner self.

Affect: Mood; feeling attached to an object, idea, or thought. The term includes inner feelings and their external manifestations.

Aftercare: The continuing program of rehabilitation designed to reinforce the effects of therapy and to help the individual adjust to the environment.

Aggression: Forceful, goal-directed behavior that may be verbal or physical.

Agitation: State of anxiety associated with severe motor restlessness.

Alienation: A feeling of detachment from oneself or society; the avoidance of emotional experiences; the efforts to estrange oneself from one's own feelings.

Ambivalence: Strong and often overwhelming simultaneous attitudes, ideas, feelings, and drives, both toward and away from an object, person, or goal.

Anorexia Nervosa: Severe weight loss brought about by the refusal to eat.

Anxiety: Mingled feelings of dread and apprehension about the future without a specific cause for fear.

APA: American Psychological Association; also American Psychiatric Association.

Apathy: Lack of feeling or mood; lack of interest and emotional involvement in one's surroundings.

Assessment: The process of determining an individual's strengths, problems, and needs. It is an ongoing process, utilizing diagnostic evaluation and progress information from involved services.

Attitude: Preparatory mental posture with which one receives stimuli and reacts to them.

Autism: When referring to schizophrenic conditions, a process that relates to retreat from reality into one's own thoughts and fantasies; a severe disorder of childhood characterized by withdrawal and lack of communication.

Bedlam: The name given to the first mental hospital founded in Europe.

Body Language: The expression of thoughts and feelings by means of bodily actions and posture.

Bulimia: Weight loss or control through forced vomiting of food, or cycles of food gorging followed by severe dieting or fasting, alone or combined.

Catharsis: Release of ideas, thoughts, and repressed materials from the unconscious, accompanied by an affective emotional response and release of tension.

Circadian Rhythm: Cyclical variations in emotional and physiologic functions that occur in 24-hour cycles.

Client Centered: A system of psychotherapy based on the assumption that the client or subject is in the best position to resolve his or her own problems.

Community Mental Health (CMH): Introduced in the 1960s by applying public health concepts and strategies to mental health services based in local centers.

Compensation: Conscious or unconscious defense mechanism by which a person tries to make up for an imagined or real deficiency, physical or psychological, or both.

Compulsion: An uncontrollable impulse to perform an act, often repetitively.

Confidentiality: Containing or keeping private information uncovered or produced in conjunction with a professional relationship.

Conflict: The simultaneous occurrence of two or more mutually antagonistic impulses or motives.

Confusion: Disturbance of consciousness manifested by a disordered orientation in relation to time, place, or person.

Conscious: Characterizing awareness or knowing; able to respond to stimulation.

Consistency: An agreement or harmony of parts or features to one another or a whole. The first of five factors in the COUNT system: The practitioner needs to be reliable and extremely consistent while working with the emotionally disturbed individual.

Coping Mechanisms: Unconscious or conscious ways of dealing with stress without changing one's goals.

COUNT System: A system designed to assist those working with the emotionally disturbed.

Countertransference: Emotions aroused within the practitioner as the result of the disturbed individual's influence on his or her own unconscious.

Creativity: Ability to produce something new.

Decompensate: The process whereby a person begins to lose control over the ability to cope with stresses of the emotions and thinking.

Defense Mechanism: Behavior patterns that maintain self-respect and/or reduce anxiety.

Deinstitutionalization: The "emptying out" of the state mental hospitals; a process begun in the 1950s with the introduction of psychotropic medications.

Delusion: Patently false beliefs held onto because the beliefs provide some type of emotional coping, support, or shelter.

Dependency: Reliance on another for psychological support. It reflects needs for security, love, protection, and mothering.

Deviant: Departure from what is considered normal, correct, or standard.

DSS: Department of Social Services.

Ego: In Freudian theory, the psychic component of the mind that mediates between the id and reality.

Electro Convulsive Therapy (ECT): The administering of an electric shock to the emotionally disturbed individual.

Empathy: Imagining the reactions, thoughts, or feelings of another person or object.

Endogenous: Produced from within or caused by factors within the organism.

Euphoria: Extreme emotional high; a feeling of well-being.

Ethics: A set of moral principles or values dealing with what is good and bad, right and wrong, conforming to accepted professional standards of conduct.

Exorcism: The ritualistic casting out of evil spirits believed to have invaded possessed persons.

Experience: Any perception, thought, memory, emotion.

Faith Healing: Treatment entirely mediated through hope and conviction.

Favoritism: A special preference given to one person or group over others.

Fear: Unpleasurable feeling or psychological changes in response to a threat or danger.

Feedback: Response; information about the state or effect of an action or a response.

Flight of Ideas: Rapid succession of thoughts without logical connections.

Folk-Support System: The people and organizations that give and receive support within a community. The four components of the folk-support system are the social, ecological, economic, and value systems.

Freud, Sigmund: The father of the psychodynamic theory.

GA: General Assistance.

GED: General Equivalency Diploma, high school level.

Genetics: The study of how traits are passed on to succeeding generations.

Gestalt Therapy: The theory that the proper subject matter for psychology is behavior and experience studied as wholes.

Goal: A broad statement of the desired condition to be achieved. Usually, goals will be long-range in nature, but scope rather than duration is their distinguishing characteristic. A goal represents the general aim of motivating behavior.

Group Dynamics: Study of group organization processes and structure.

Guilt: Feelings associated with self-reproachment and need for punishment.

Hallucination: An apparent perception, but with no corresponding stimuli present and not shared by others.

Homeostasis: A tendency of biological systems to maintain the stability optimal for survival through continually adjusting to conditions that alter this balance.

Id: According to Freud, the mass of biological drives with which the individual is born.

Impulse: Unexpected, instinctive urge motivated by conscious and unconscious feelings over which the person has little or no control.

Impotency: Male sexual disorder characterized by the inability to begin the physical act of intercourse.

Insecurity: Feelings of helplessness and inadequacy in the face of anxiety about one's place, one's future, and one's goals.

Insomnia: Inability to sleep.

Instinct: Unlearned goal-oriented actions.

IQ: Intelligence Quotient; a standardized measure of intellectual functioning.

Isolation: Withdrawal from others.

Judgment: Mental act of comparing or evaluating choices within the framework of a given set of values for the purpose of electing a course of action.

Metabolize: The chemical changes in living cells, by which energy is provided for vital processes and activities.

Moral Treatment: A treatment procedure developed in the early nineteenth century based on treating individuals with kindness and respect.

Naturalness: Freedom from pretension or calculation. The fourth of five factors in the COUNT system. The worker needs to be oneself while working with the emotionally disturbed.

Nervous Breakdown: An inaccurate description of emotional disturbance.

Neurologist: A medical physician (M.D.) who specializes in diseases of the central nervous system.

Neurosis: A mental disorder characterized by anxiety. The anxiety may be experienced and expressed directly, or, through an unconscious psychic process, it may be converted, displaced, or somatized.

Norms: Standards of action that specify what behavior is expected and what behavior is not.

Optimism: An inclination to put the most favorable construction upon actions and events or to anticipate the best possible outcome. The second of five factors in the COUNT system. The worker needs to instill a sense of hope in the disturbed individual.

OT: Occupational therapist or occupational therapy.

Paranoia: A psychosis characterized by a complicated, highly elaborate delusional system, which often is developed logically from the distortion of a real event.

Pinel, Philippe: A French physician who introduced what he and others called *moral treatment*.

Potentiation: Enhancement of one agent by another so that the combined effect is greater than the sum of the effects of each one alone.

Prefrontal Lobotomy: A surgical procedure in which a cut is made between the frontal lobes of the brain.

Prejudice: Prejudgments that cause people to act in a certain way toward members of a particular group.

Psychoanalysis: A dynamic system of psychology that seeks the roots of human behavior in unconscious motivation and conflict.

Psychodynamic Theory: A theory that conceptualizes the human psyche as an interaction of three forces: id, the ego, and the superego.

Psychosis: A severe emotional disorder characterized by a break with reality manifested in disorganization of the thought processes, disturbance in emotion, disorientation as to time, space, and person, and in some cases hallucinations and delusions.

Psychotherapy: The application of specialized techniques to the treatment of emotional disorders or to the problems of everyday adjustment.

Psychotropic Medications: Medicines designed to help in the treatment of the emotionally disturbed.

Reinforcement: Anything increasing the probability of eliciting a learned response.

Schizophrenia: A general name for a group of psychotic reactions characterized by withdrawal, disturbance in emotion and feeling, hallucinations, and delusions.

Self-Fulfilling Prophecy: A belief, prediction, or expectation that serves to bring about its own fulfillment.

Significant Other: Members of an individual's support system; those who have a close relationship with the person; family members, lovers, close friends.

Social Role: The pattern of behavior that characterizes, and that others expect of, a person who occupies a particular status or position in a social situation.

SSA: Social Security Administration.

SSI: Supplemental Security Income.

Stereotype: Preconceived notions, often having no rational basis, about how particular people or groups act.

Superego: In Freudian theory, that part of the mind in which the individual has incorporated the moral standards of the society.

Theory: Contemplation; speculation; the analysis of a set of facts in their ideal relations to one another.

Therapist: An individual trained in the treatment of emotional disorders.

Toxin: A harmful or poisonous substance.

Transference: Emotions aroused within the individual that develop as a result of a relationship, especially a therapeutic relationship.

Trustworthiness: The ability to rely on the character, ability, strength, or truth of someone or something. The fifth factor in the COUNT system. The development of trust is the goal in the developing relationship with the emotionally disturbed individual.

Unbiased Attitude: Freedom from all prejudice and favoritism. The third of five factors in the COUNT system. The practitioner needs to be without prejudice or favoritism while working with the emotionally disturbed.

Unconscious: Characterizing an activity for which the individual does not know the reason or motive for the act.

REFERENCES

About Schizophrenia (1981). South Deerfield, Mass.: Channing L. Bete.

American Psychiatric Association (1980). *Diagnostic and Statistical Manual of Mental Disorders.* 3rd ed. Washington, D.C. Known as DSM III.

American Psychological Association (1981). Ethical Principles of Psychologists. *The American Psychologist* 36, no. 6, 633–638.

Atwood, G. (1972). Note on a Relationship between Suicidal Intentions and the Depressive Mood. *Psychotherapy: Theory, Research, and Practice* 9:284–285.

Bates, M. M., & Johnson, C. D. (1972). *Group Leadership.* Denver: Love Publishing.

Balwin, B. A. (1979). Crisis Intervention: An Overview of Therapy and Practice. *The Counseling Psychologist* 8:43–52.

Barchas, J. D. (1977). *Psychopharmacology from Theory to Practice.* England: Oxford University Press.

Bateson, G., Jackson, D., Haley, J., & Weakland, A. (1956). Toward a Theory of Schizophrenia. *Behavioral Science* 1:251–264.

Beels, C. (1978). Family and Social Management of Schizophrenia. In P. Guerin Jr. (Ed.), *Family Therapy—Theory and Practice.* New York: Gardner Press.

Buss, A. (1966). *Psychotherapy.* New York: John Wiley and Sons.

Calhoun, J. F. (1977). *Abnormal Psychology Current Perspectives.* 2nd ed. New York: Random House.

Commission on Professional and Hospital Activities (1978). *International Classification of Diseases.* 9th rev., Clinical Modification. Ann Arbor, Mich.: Edwards Brothers.

Daves, W. (1975). *A Textbook of General Psychology.* New York: Thomas Y. Crowell.

Diedrich, R. C., & Dye, H. A. (1972). *Group Procedures: Purpose, Processes, & Outcomes.* Boston: Houghton Mifflin.

Durkheim, E. (1951). *Suicide: A Study in Sociology.* New York: Free Press.

Erikson, E. H. (1950). *Childhood and Society.* New York: Norton.

Evans, D. (1983). *The Lives of Mentally Retarded People.* Boulder, Colo.: Westview Press.

Farberow, N. L., Helif, S. M., & Litman, R. E. (1970). *The Psychology of Suicide.* New York: Science House.

Foucault, M. (1965). *Madness and Civilization.* New York: Random House.
Freedman, A. M., Kaplan, H. I., & Sadock, B. J. (Eds.) (1976). *Modern Synopsis of Psychiatry II.* Baltimore: Williams and Wilkins.
Freud, S. (1957). *The Future Prospects of Psycho-Analytic Therapy.* Standard Edition. London: Hogarth Press. 11:139–151.

Giampa, F. L., Walker-Burt, G., & Finger, C. (Eds.) (1983). *Group Home Curriculum.* Lansing, Mich.: Michigan Department of Mental Health.
Goldstein, A. P. (1962). *Therapist–Patient Expectancies in Psychotherapy.* New York: Pergamon Press.

Halpern, H. A. (1973). Crisis Theory: A Definitional Study. *Community Mental Health Journal* 9:342–349.
Hammond, D. C., & Stanfield, K. (1977). Common Misconceptions about Self, World, Goals, and Ideals. *Multidimensional Psychotherapy: A Counselor's Guide for the Map Form.* Champaign, Ill.: Institute for Personality and Ability Testing.
Hobbs, N. (1964). Mental Health's Third Revolution. *American Journal of Orthopsychiatry* 34:822–833.
Holmes, T. H., & Rahe, R. H. (1967). The Social Readjustment Scale. *Journal of Psychosomatic Research* 11, no. 2, 213–218.
Homans, G. C. (1950). The Human Group: An Overview of Dynamics of Group Development. *HarBrace Journal,* 112–113.

Kallman, F. (1953). *Heredity and Health in Mental Disorders.* New York: Norton.
Karon, B. P., & Vandenbos, G. R. (1981). *Psychotherapy of Schizophrenia.* New York: Jason Aronson.
Kline, N. S. (1974). *From Sad to Glad.* New York: Ballantine Books.

Laing, R. D. (1972). *The Politics of the Family and Other Essays.* New York: Random House.
Leigh, D., & Pare, C. (Eds.) (1977). *A Concise Encyclopedia of Psychiatry.* Baltimore: John Marks University Press.
Lidz, T. (1973). *The Origin and Treatment of Schizophrenic Disorders.* New York: Basic Books.

Mendel, W. M. (1979). Staff Burnout: Diagnosis, Treatment, and Prevention. *New Directions for Mental Health Services* 2:75–83.
Michigan Department of Mental Health and Social Services. *Adult Foster Care Providers Manual.* Publication #260. Lansing, Mich.
Miller, T. (Ed.) (1973). *Theories of Psychopathology and Personality: Essays and Critiques.* Philadelphia: W. B. Sanders.
Mora, F. H. (1982). Therapist Burnout and The Chronic Client (or the Story of Rescuing). *Proceedings of the Annual Conference on Partial Hospitalization, 1981.* Boston, Mass.: The American Association for Partial Hospitalization.

Paykel, E. S. (Ed.) (1982). *Handbook of Affective Disorders.* New York: The Guilford Press.
Perls, F. S. (1969). *Gestalt Therapy Verbatim.* LaFayette, Calif.: Real People Press.
Physicians' Desk Reference. New York: C. E. Baker, published annually.

Ratner, S. C. (1975). Animals' Defenses: Fighting in Predatory Relations. In Pliner, Krames, & Alloway (Eds.), *Nonverbal Communication of Aggression*. New York: Plenum.
—— (1967). Comparative Aspects of Hypnosis. In J. E. Gordon (Ed.), *Handbook of Clinical and Experimental Hypnosis*. New York: Macmillan.
Rogers, C. R. (1983). *Freedom to Learn for the '80s*. Columbus, Ohio: Charles E. Merrill.
Rosenthal, R., & Jacobson, L. (1968). *Pygmalion in the Classroom*. New York: Holt, Rinehart and Winston.

Schwebel, M. (1955). Why Unethical Practice? *Journal of Counseling Psychology* 2:122–128.
Slaikeu, K. A. (1984). *Crisis Intervention: A Handbook for Practice and Research*. Boston: Allyn and Bacon.
Starr, P. (1982). *The Social Transformation of American Medicine*. New York: Basic Books.
Steiner, C. M. (1974). *Scripts People Live*. New York: Grove Press.
Suinn, R. (1970). *Fundamentals of Behavior Pathology*. New York: Wiley Press.
Svoboda, W. (1979). *Learning About Epilepsy*. Washington, D.C.: University Park Press.

Van Hoose, W. H., & Kottler, J. A. (1982). *Ethical and Legal Issues in Counseling and Psychotherapy*. San Francisco: Jossey-Bass Publishers.

Welch, D. I., Medeiros, G. C., & Tate, G. A. (1982). *Beyond Burnout: How to Enjoy Your Job Again When You've Just About Had Enough*. New York: Prentice-Hall.
Whaley, D., & Malott, R. (1968). *Elementary Principles of Behavior*. Englewood Cliffs, N.J.: Prentice-Hall.
Wolman, B., Egan, J., & O'Ross, A. (Eds.) (1953). *Handbook of Treatment of Mental Disorders in Childhood and Adolescence*. Englewood Cliffs, N.J.: Prentice-Hall.

Yalom, I. D. (1983). *Inpatient Group Psychotherapy*. New York: Basic Books, 1983.

Zilboorg, G., & Henry, G. W. (1941). *A History of Medical Psychology*. New York: Norton.

SUGGESTED FURTHER READINGS

Castaneda, C. (1971). *A Separate Reality: Further Conversations with Don Juan.* New York: Simon and Schuster.

Greenberg, J. (1964). *I Never Promised You a Rose Garden.* New York: Holt, Rinehart and Winston.

Hesse, H. (1929). *Steppenwolf.* New York: Holt, Rinehart and Winston.

Jung, C. G. (1961). *Memories, Dreams, Reflections.* New York: Random House.

Kesey, K. (1962). *One Flew Over The Cuckoo's Nest.* New York: Viking Press.

Kopp, S. B. (1972). *If You Meet the Buddha on the Road, Kill Him!: The Pilgrimage of Psychotherapy Patients.* New York: Bantam Books.

Laing, R. D. (1967). *The Politics of Experience.* New York: Ballantine Books.

Perls, F. S. (1972). *In and out the Garbage Pail.* New York: Bantam Books.

Silverman, H. M., & Simon, G. I. (1981). *The Pill Book.* New York: Bantam Books.

Stern, E. L. (1975). *Prescription Drugs and Their Side Effects.* New York: Grosset and Dunlap.

Szasz, T. S. (1974). *The Myth of Mental Illness.* New York: Harper and Row.

Vonnegut, M. (1975). *The Eden Express.* New York: Bantam Books.

INDEX

Advanced daily living skills, 134–35; examples of, 135
Affect, flat, 47; inappropriate, 47
Affective disorders, 42–44
Aggression, 176; staff response to, 176–78
Akathisia. *See* Medication, side effects and
Anti-social personality, 38–40
Art therapy, 141–44; examples of, 144
Asylums, 21–22

Baseball therapy, 182; caution for, 182, 183
Basic trust, 117, 118
Bateson, G., 62
Bedlam, 21, 22
Beels, C., 48
Behavior modification, 65–67. *See also* Human rights
Behavior therapy, 96, 97; punishment and, 97. *See also* Human rights
Biology, 60, 61
Blueler, E., 57
Blocking, 46
Body, in relation to mind, 69, 70
Brainstorming, 133, 134
Burnout, 187; causes and symptoms of, 187–91; the paradoxical nature of, 188–89; prevention of, 188–92

Catatonia, 49
Cholinergic blockers, 77; in preventing medication side effects, 77
Circadian rhythms, 58

Classical conditioning (respondent), 66
Commitment, 96; procedures of, 96. *See also* Human rights
Community awareness, 135, 136; examples of, 136, 137
Community Mental Health (CMH), 22, 26–29
Community Mental Health Centers Act, 26
Community placement, 28
Confidentiality, 92, 93; definition of, 92; examples of violations, 93; intentional breach of, 92. *See also* Human rights
Consistency, 104; in COUNT System, 103; countertransference and, 107–9; examples of, 105, 106; physical intervention and, 106; the practitioner and, 106, 107; in relation to schizophrenia, 104, 105; transference and, 106
COUNT System, 101; definition of, 103, 104
Countertransference, 106–8
Crime and mental illness, 58
Crisis intervention, 146; depression and, 156, 157; distorted thinking and (chart), 158, 159; emergency procedures, 166, 167; follow-up, 169, 170; goals of, 146, 150, 168; motivation for change, 168, 169; precipitating factors, 147–50; problem solving during, 167, 168; three factors in, 152–56
Cycles of the body, 58, 59

The authors all are limited licensed clinical psychologists in the state of Michigan. Jonathan P. Beard is employed at Detroit Osteopathic Hospital Psychiatric Services. David L. Hayter is employed at the Macomb Oakland Regional Center for the Michigan Department of Mental Health. Eric Shenkar is employed at a partial hospitalization program for St. Clair County, Michigan Community Mental Health Services.

The manuscript was edited by Gnomi Gouldin. The book was designed by Joanne Elkin Kinney. The typeface for the text and the display type is Times Roman. The book is printed on 55-lb. Glatfelter text paper. The cloth edition is bound in Holliston Mills' Roxite Linen.

Manufactured in the United States of America.